IS THAT EVEN A COUNTRY, SIR!

Journeys in Northeast India by Train, Bus and Tractor

ANIL YADAV

Translated from the Hindi by
ANURAG BASNET

SPEAKING
TIGER

SPEAKING TIGER PUBLISHING PVT. LTD
4381/4, Ansari Road, Daryaganj
New Delhi 110002

Copyright © Anil Yadav 2012
This translation copyright © Anurag Basnet 2017

Originally published in Hindi by Antika Prakashan in 2012
Published in English by Speaking Tiger in paperback 2017

ISBN: 978-93-86582-33-1 / eISBN 978-86582-32-4

10 9 8 7 6 5 4 3 2 1

Typeset in Adobe Garamond Pro by SÜRYA, New Delhi
Printed at Thomson Press India Ltd.

All rights reserved.
No part of this publication may be reproduced,
transmitted, or stored in a retrieval system,
in any form or by any means, electronic,
mechanical, photocopying, recording
or otherwise, without the prior
permission of the publisher.

This book is sold subject to the condition that it shall not,
by way of trade or otherwise, be lent, resold,
hired out, or otherwise circulated, without the
publisher's prior consent, in any form of
binding or cover other than that in
which it is published.

IS THAT EVEN A COUNTRY, SIR!

~

PRAISE FOR THE BOOK

'By unveiling the Northeast both in intense detail and in its most essential form, Anil Yadav has given readers the ability to see India in its widest breadth. The Northeast is a neglected and little-known part of the country; to view it only through the prism of beauty is incomplete. Journeying over difficult roads, Anil has brought together information and knowledge, adventure and narrative, storytelling and reportage to fashion a unique travelogue.'

—Gyanranjan, editor, *Pahal*

'A gripping and informative book; it reminded me of the old travel memoirs which I have read—*Papillon* with its indomitable protagonist Henri Charrière ... Mohan Rakesh's *Aakhri Chattan Tak* ... and the works of [Rahul] Sankrityayan.'

—Rajendra Yadav, *Hans*

'Anil Yadav very effectively communicates the grief, oppression, infiltration, the politics of migration, governmental neglect and militancy of the Northeast ... This book is an important reminder that the Northeast is a wounded part of independent India, and any attempt to heal it needs an iron will.'

—*Jansatta*

'The story of India's most neglected region told by the narrative voice of a poor, petulant reporter... Stripped of the exotic, the Northeast in [this book] appears bare, burnt and betrayed.'

—Scroll.in

'As much a book about the North East as ... a discourse on fundamental elements like land and language that constitute our identity. [Anil Yadav's] voice is fresh, his style hardcore, his language mellifluous.'

—Scroll.in

Author's dedication:

*For Tipu,
who circles the earth with his toy truck*

Seeing the soiled Brahmaputra Mail standing at the terrifyingly dirty, stinking, crowded Platform Number 9 of the Old Delhi Railway Station, I thought, This train has been standing here forever. It will never move.

Streaks of dried, crusted vomit were gleaming on the broken windows of the darkened coaches. Rats of a size between mongoose and cat were fearlessly roaming on the tracks. 29 November 2000; that night, all the exposed parts of our bodies were stinging with mosquito bites. At first glance, there was only one simple conclusion to be drawn: This train was standing forlorn in the darkness because it was travelling to the most mysterious and neglected part of the country.

It was to catch this defeated train that Anhes Shashwat and I had darted out like arrows half an hour earlier from our rented room in East Delhi. I had shouted at the taxi-driver all the way to the railway station so that we wouldn't miss the Mail. My haversack-strap had snapped in the rush and I was having to make do with a crude knot. This was the haversack which my friend Shahid Raza and his friend Lakshmi Pant, a journalist, had found at a roadside-vendor's that same morning and bought, along with a cheap sleeping bag.

I knew nothing about the Northeast.

My father had once been posted at the Dibrugarh Airbase. It was in the Northeast that a relative, visiting on business, had drowned in the Brahmaputra and died. His money-filled bag had fallen into the river and, in trying to retrieve it, the steamer's railing had slipped from his grasp. Some people from my maternal village once worked on a farm in a district of Assam. Their children had told me that men in Assam are called kela—for banana, and also an expletive. From the pictures in the Social Science and Geography textbooks of my childhood, I knew there are tea gardens in the Northeast where women pluck leaves from bushes. Once upon a time the women there used to turn outsiders into sheep through magic and keep them as pets. Also that there was some place called Cherrapunjee where it rained the most in the world.

Apart from this information, I knew a little about the student revolution of Assam. I knew, especially, that in the final years of the 1980s, hotshot student leaders of Benares used to shout themselves hoarse into microphones: 'If this Prafulla Kumar Mahanta, resident of this room in that hostel in Guwahati, can become chief minister of Assam, why can't we students write our own destinies in our own blood?' To gather a crowd before such meetings, these students, boys as well as girls, would sing the Hindi version of Bhupen Hazarika's song: 'O Ganga, why do you flow?'

Pankaj Srivastav, who too sang this song at one point in time, had given me a plain, one-year-old diary (which he himself must have got at a press conference) in which I was to record my memoirs. I also had a little more than half a kilogramme of newspaper-cuttings and two books (*India's Northeast Resurgent* by B.G. Verghese and Sanjoy Hazarika's *Strangers of the Mist*) which I had to read on the train over the next three days. I had bought these books a day earlier from a glittering store in Connaught Place, without asking for a discount, and had paid for them with Shashwat's credit card. I also had the warm clothes which had been bought from the roadside market on Janpath nearby. From that same market I had purchased a bright red jacket that looked like an overcoat and had presented it to Shashwat, duly dry-cleaned and neatly packaged. After having avoided Shashwat's questions a number of times, I had told him that the jacket had cost nine-thousand-and-something rupees when it had actually been bought for three hundred. Wearing that jacket, Shashwat was now sitting on a bench on the platform squeezing Otrivin into his nostrils, the nasal drop usually prescribed for children. His nose would be frequently stuffy in winter. From time to time, he would dig into his pockets for patti and nibble it. He was convinced that after the dispatches and the photographs we sent from the Northeast to the magazines and papers in Delhi were published, we would shine bright as comets in the night sky. We would finally be liberated from our forced, annual, humiliating visits to incompetent and arrogant editors, begging for jobs. Some blank foolscap-sized notebooks, as well as the parathas, the fried fish and the pickle which our kind landlady in East Delhi had packed for us, were locked away in Shashwat's attaché.

I had been unemployed for a year; Shashwat, for five months. There were many mornings when he would be walking out softly, formally dressed, to visit newspaper proprietors and editors. I would fling my quilt aside and stand before him. Theatrically, I would tell him how, in running after a measly job, he looked like an orphaned stray dog loping after a Delhi Transport Corporation bus. His courage, gathered in solitude, would dissipate with a hollow laugh and the job-hunt would be suspended. I had myself been a victim of depression. That year I had set records in sleeping up to eighteen hours at a stretch, under a yellow sheet in summer and under a quilt in winter. This journey was beginning with the desire to shake off depression and with a dim ray of hope in the fog of uncertainty that shrouded the impulse to find myself once more.

I had no idea what I would do in the Northeast.

So I had put an imaginary question to the authors Khushwant Singh, Rajendra Yadav, Prabhash Joshi, Mangalesh Dabral, Anand Swarup Verma, Rajendra Dhodpakar, Abhay Kumar Dubey, Yashwant Vyas, Ramsharan Joshi, Rambahadur Rai, Arvind Jain and noted their answers on a piece of paper. 'Sir! Suppose you were to visit that region these days, what would you see, and what would you write about?'

To this flighty question, I received answers that were as flimsy as paper airplanes. It was these answers which I had kneaded and pounded to work up Shashwat's and my confidence enough to board the train. According to the editor of *Hans* magazine, Rajendra Yadav, it would be better for me to have a woman for a travelling companion. He thought I would have better luck understanding the society of the region and there would be some hype in the media, too. But it was Khushwant Singh who gave me the most straightforward counsel in his realistic style. I reached his house merely half an hour after the appointed time and was told a meeting wasn't possible. When I called from a PCO (Public Call Office) nearby, the old Sardar, sipping whisky, answered, 'Boy, you go to the Northeast or anywhere else... What do I care?'

On my sheet of answers, I wrote against Khushwant Singh's name: 'You must go, son. There are very few people who can dare this. I will help you place your travelogue in English with publishers such as Penguin or Viking.'

This reply was meant for Shashwat since he was financing the trip. As I repeated Khushwant Singh's words to myself like a benediction, I thought of my younger brother Sunil. As children, when I would grow tired of carrying him around on my bicycle, he would sense my fatigue and say, 'The two men who were passing by were talking amongst themselves. One said, "This boy rides his bicycle like it is an aeroplane."' I wouldn't be able to see his face since he would be sitting on the crossbar in front of me.

~

When we entered the coach, having braved the melee after the first boarding whistle went off, we found some Mongoloid-featured soldiers of the Assam Rifles stowing away their luggage. They were fitting their trunks, kitbags, holdalls and haversacks into corners and gaps with such silent, detached efficiency, it seemed as if those spaces had been specially moulded for those articles.

A young Sardar who had already laid out his bed on an overhead berth was explaining to the person who had come to see him off that his seat was actually in an adjoining coach but a Naga man was on the berth opposite him. According to the Sardar, this man stank terribly and so he had asked the ticket-examiner to have his seat changed.

Who knows what problem the young Sardar had had with that Naga man? Maybe the Naga's slitted eyes, which could pierce through to his innermost being, had played a horror movie—featuring head-hunting, dog-meat-and-rice, and militancy—on the screen of his mind and the young man had been forced to come and sink into the secure quicksand of those beaten-down Biharis who were returning to their des—their country—after having earned some money in Delhi. On a bus in Delhi, he probably wouldn't allow them to even touch him because, in Delhi, the word 'Bihari' is an insult.

The train inched forward and stopped. 'One name echoes in the heavens and on earth resounds—Ram Vilas Paswan!' A crowd of young Bihari men, each one a pale photocopy of youth, entered the coach shouting this slogan. They started to bind themselves to the side berths using their cheap attachés, their Delhi-model two-in-ones and the colourful clothes they had bought from the footpaths of the city. The passengers with reserved seats fortified their berths with luggage and began to occupy space. They were using their body language to protest against these ticketless Dalit party-workers who were returning from a rally.

Two ticket-examiners entered the coach. They asked a feeble lungi-clad boy for his ticket. The boy kept staring at them with scared yellow eyes. Before he could say a word, one of the officials slapped him hard and began pushing everyone out of the coach. A bearded young man talked back: 'Mister! We've come from Paswanji's rally. Why should we buy tickets? We will travel back home the same way we came.'

'Ask them how they dare enter this coach.' A voice came from a distant berth.

'Our houses are vacant, come and occupy them. Go, get money from Paswan, reserve seats and then sit here.' The two ticket-examiners completely prevailed over the young men. 'Paswan is not the rail minister anymore. He can do nothing to us now. Son, we are leaders of the Railway Trade Union; we can throw each one of you down and beat you. And even the public will soon show you your Paswan's worth. Now get off.'

The Dalit youth quietly got off the coach and headed over to the general compartment like they were walking in a funeral procession. The power of politics and organization had given them courage to board the train without buying tickets; the ticket-examiners had used that same power to force them off it. It is only the Dalits upon whom the ticket-examiners unleash their fists. When the Jats of Baghpat and Muzaffarnagar travel to rallies called by the Bharatiya Kisan Union, they board air-conditioned coaches without tickets and tear down even the window-curtains to smoke in their chillums. Then these ticket-examiners find corners to cower in and tremble for their lives and their jobs.

The train moved on. The soldiers opened their bottles. They began drinking rum out of mugs and disposable plastic glasses. Their silence broke, too. Long-drawn-out laughter in alien tongues merged into each other and swirled about inside the coach. People travelling with families became alert. Those sitting on the berths near the soldiers slid in the opposite direction, even if it was by mere inches. A middle-aged constable of the GRP (Government Railway Police) gestured to the soldiers and started to say something but, finding no response, moved on grumbling. This was Mongol India, whose dialogue with an Aryan soldier from the Gangetic plains would prove difficult.

The name of a downy-moustached bearer who kept making trips into the coach from the pantry-car presented a challenge to one's weather-related knowledge. Pinned to his red cotton uniform was a black name-tag upon which was written in white alphabets: Sajal Baishakh—literally, the drenched month of Baishakh. As I looked at his slitted eyes and clean white teeth, a thought struck me: The rains begin in the month of Ashadh, how can the month of Baishakh be drenched? Had he been so named only to astonish people? At breakfast the following morning, I asked him, 'How did Baishakh become sajal?' He laughed contentedly for a long time. Then came a counter-question: 'Are you going to Assam for the first time?' When I nodded, he replied, 'If you stay there for some days you will know; in Baishakh, not only monsoon, flood also comes.' This was my first glimpse of the Northeast, which I caught somewhere between Mughalsarai and Bihar.

I found that the imposing Mustachio who overbearingly encroached upon my berth in the daytime was from my district, Ghazipur. Virendra Singh of Gahmar village. After a furlough of fiteen days, he was going back to Bongaigaon in Lower Assam where he was part of a Border Security Force (BSF) battalion. It could be that Virendra belonged to the same district as mine, or that he wanted to legitimize his encroachment upon my space; he thrust a palmful of chewing tobacco towards me and counselled, 'Now that you're on your way, avoid the women and the mosquitoes there. Only then can you return to Ghazipur. Damn! Is that even a country, Sir?' This was his catchphrase.

He told me that in the BSF, personnel are made to line up, struck on their mouths and forced to swallow quinine tablets. There is also a standing order that they should sleep inside mosquito nets; there is a fine for defying that order. Life is always fragile, as if it were suspended upon a leaf, because who knows when the ULFA and Bodo wallas will arrive and start shooting. Militants freely roam among crowds of people, he said, like fish in water. Their presence would be known only after a few people were gunned down.

Like fish in water—I was astonished by Mustachio's simile. This was precisely the phrase written in the book by Sanjoy Hazarika, that same Sanjoy Hazarika who had studied English at St Edmund's College in Shillong and journalism in London. The commander of the United Liberation Front of Assam (ULFA), Paresh Baruah, once mingled with a college football team in Tinsukia, participated in their match against the Assam Police team, and made his escape. By the time the police came to know of this three days later, all the ULFA camps in the nearby jungles had been dismantled.

On the berth opposite me was a sahuain surrounded by about fifteen airbags, sacks and polythene packets. Her husband, the sahu, had a seat in some other coach. After every two hours she would say, 'Bhaiya, keep a lookout, my two girls are with me.' The family had a grocery store in Moreh, the final outpost on Indian territory on the border with Burma.

'How did you reach Moreh from Gorakhpur?'

'Destiny, Bhaiya.'

Her two daughters, one eight, the other eleven, attended a government school and spoke a unique kind of English. They would call each other 'man'. The sahuain would encourage her daughters in her wordless way and survey the impact they were having on the rest of the coach with satisfaction.

'Mamma gave me only three taka to take jhalmuri. Why should I give that to you? Take from your money, man.'

The sahuain told Mustachio, 'Small small boys without beards or moustaches come, in front of military, police, everyone. Ask for tax. We have to give. Or they will kill. Shot a schoolmaster in front of our store. He was a gentleman. He spoke nicely with everyone but hadn't paid tax for three months. They have stopped us from speaking our language. They say speak any language but don't speak Hindi. If we make mistake and our tongue slips they abuse.' So this unique English was a language which had been innovated by the children of outsiders living on the Indo-Burma border so that they could stay alive.

'Leave, then. Go back to Gorakhpur and run a grocery store there.' Shashwat advised drowsily from inside his sleeping bag.

'No, Bhaiya. The fun that is in Moreh cannot be found in aal-India.'

'Damn! Is that even a country, Sir?'

~

Mustachio's 'des' is not that country which used to be pointed out to us in the political maps of the Geography textbooks of our childhood. Nor is his 'des' that country which the prime minister addresses on 15 August from the Red Fort. As a matter of fact, he was travelling from his des—his country—to 'pardes'—abroad—to work there.

Photographs from some of the press cuttings stuffed

in my haversack danced before my eyes. On them were images of slogans which had been written in an artistic hand.

'Indian dogs go back'—where were those dogs which were chasing the Indian dogs out of their territory?

'Delhi is stepmother to Seven Sisters'—which girls were these seven sisters taunting?

'As crow flies, it is closer to Hanoi than to Delhi'— why was it being said that we have settled by mistake in a neighbourhood of Delhiwallas?

All at once I thought, If the people from 'there' are steadily abusing the people from 'here', this train, travelling there, must surely be saying something too. I shut my eyes and tried to listen to all the sounds. Since the day before, useless, futile fragments of sentences had been wandering about in the coach in the cold, rustling wind, accompanied by the clackety-clack of the onrushing train. They were being repeated ad infinitum. What were the intentions behind such emotionally charged sentences being spoken in a variety of ways?

Situation is very bad.

The position there isn't good at all.

The atmosphere is vitiated.

It is an all-around mess.

There's an uproar again nowadays.

It was as if people were talking about the condition of a violent lunatic with whom they had to share a hospital ward.

~

We had crossed Bihar. Scenes from a Satyajit Ray film were unfolding outside the windows. The villages of Malda in Bengal were passing by in front of our eyes. Plain houses, bordered by green ponds enveloped in greenery; paddy fields with crops, some standing, some harvested—everything was domed by a blue sky that stretched to the horizon. On the train, sweet curd, jhalmuri and handloom cloth were being sold.

As soon as we reached New Jalpaiguri, NJP, we took off from rural Bengal and fell into a foreign lane filled with Chinese-made goods. Hundreds of vendors came one after another screaming their wares: cameras, televisions, calculators, mobiles, phones, watches, tape-recorders, electronic toys, blankets and balm—all made in China. Laden from head to toe with products, they were looking like business ambassadors for China. All the cigarettes being sold on the platform were foreign-made—longer than the cigarettes manufactured in India, and cheaper. The Chinese ambassadors were so many that beggars, carrying their sarangis and ektaras, couldn't board the train.

In the language of politics, NJP is termed the 'Chicken's Neck Corridor'. This passage is a 21-kilometre-wide strip of land which carries oil and gas pipelines from the Northeast. The militants of the Northeast frequently threaten to wring this chicken's neck. If this were to happen, not only would the supplies of oil and gas be severed, the Northeast, too, would be cut off from the rest of India. One would have to catch a plane just to get to Guwahati from Kolkata.

From the vendors, newspapers and mobile phones—whenever they could catch networks—news was arriving that Hindi-speakers were being killed in Assam. Houses belonging to Biharis were being torched. In Sadiya village of the Kukurmara sub-division, somewhere between

Tinsukia in Assam and Arunachal Pradesh, the ULFA had gunned down thirty Biharis. Their corpses were still rotting where they had fallen. All the victims were labourers who had been returning on a truck after making their purchases from the weekly market in Tezu. The truck had been stopped in a jungle, the labourers were all made to get off, stand in a line, and were asked for their names after which they were shot. Trains returning from the Northeast had no space in them. The Biharis were fleeing Assam, leaving behind their houses and their lands. In the last week alone, more than fifty-five Biharis had been killed.

Sanjoy Hazarika's book contained blood, gunpowder, guerillas, Muslims from Mymensingh in Bangladesh, refugees and intruders. Verghese's book had treaties, MOUs, the machinations of politics, administrative reforms and history. As I read these books and dozed, I felt that this train was full of the utterly helpless. It was taking these people to a place they didn't want to go to. Manacled by wages, by business, and by relationships, they had been forced to sit inside the train. And they were still on their way even though they knew that death danced there. All at once, the easy relaxation of a long-distance journey dissipated and a sharp alertness began to walk on talons. Barring three, all other languages and dialects set up a frightened whispering. These three languages were Assamese, English and a smattering of Bangla. I looked over at Shashwat, who was bundled up in his sleeping-bag gnawing his fingernails. After a while, he said, 'Now that our rotten fate has brought us this far, we will face whatever is to come.'

~

As your cross over into Assam, there is an explosion of green. Dark green that shines black in the sun. On windows, in the cracks on the walls of houses, from the hollows of trees, are seen green creepers which have taken over every available space. Villages surrounded by bamboo, areca-nut, coconut and banana trees which shaded moss-covered ponds and pondlets. Houses and fields were surrounded by bamboo fences. The expanse outside was covered in a bluish haze.

Small stations and halts were passing by—New Bongaigaon, Nalbari, Barpeta, Rangiya... The reports and pictures published in newspapers were all saying that these were those places where the killings of Hindi-speakers had taken place in recent days. Buying red tea and some local savouries from a vendor, it struck me that my speech is inflected with a Bihari accent which makes an appearance at unguarded moments.

'Our name is Aneel Yadav.'

I can't tell how many individuals I gather within, other than my self, when I draw out my name.

I saw a strange man who was carrying a crude bamboo flute in his hands. It cast a doubt in my mind: Does this thing even play? He was telling passengers: 'Song... listen to a song? Pay only if you like.' Such confidence in his music! I wanted to stop him but couldn't. I thought, Who knows, maybe these people are using these techniques to identify Hindi-speakers on trains.

'May I sit here only for three minutes?' A middle-aged man carrying a bag and an umbrella asked me in English. I scooted over. He explained that it takes the train three minutes to cross the bridge over the Brahmaputra. Then, Guwahati. All the windows were lined with backs. Women, muttering prayers for their lives, their belongings and their children were casting coins into the monstrous river which lay stretched out in the blue haze.

~

Both of us had an idea of where we were going and also the sort of people who were going to welcome us there.

But the first thing I wanted to do as we exited the railway station was to eat tamul—the areca-nut, eaten as a mild narcotic. Since I was a child, I have associated the emotions of fear, revulsion, guilt and attraction with tamul. It was tamul which ended the innocence of my life and took on different forms in my dreams to keep me terrorized for many days.

I must have been seven then. The neighbours in my mother's village, the ones who lived in Assam, had a visitor, a man called Pradyumna. He was the first person whom I had seen eating tamul—an egg-shaped, brown, stinking, smooth, strange object. One afternoon, I was sitting in their courtyard when Pradyumna gave me a tamul to play with. He spoke to me sweetly for a few minutes, then took hold of my small, delicate fingers, pulled them inside his dhoti and wrapped them around his hot, heavy penis. He then took the world-famous red-bordered gamcha of Assam and it. I only glimpsed it; the tip looked just like a tamul. I was stunned; my mouth open, I kept staring into his red eyes. An elderly woman of the household who was sitting nearby smoking a hookah understood what was happening. She glared, asked for the gamcha and made a move to pick it up. The man quickly let me go. I remained in a fever for two days, my left hand balled into a fist that would not unclench.

Copying others, I placed a 1-rupee coin on a tamul-vendor's cart. He gave me half a betel-leaf, half a tamul, and a big dollop of slaked lime on a piece of paper. Without waiting even a second, I popped everything into my mouth, chewed slowly first and then in earnest. In just a little while, my temples grew hot, my throat dried up, and I started pouring with sweat. One thing was certain: as long as I was travelling in the Northeast, I was going to eat tamul. It had a tremendous kick; powerful enough to uproot one from an older state and propel into a new emotional universe. Actually, I knew that in my soul is a tamul-shaped wound that eases with it being chewed, its heat released, and will fill in only once it has been spit out.

Propping our luggage on a rickshaw we spoke almost simultaneously, 'Take us to the cheapest hotel you know.' The rickshaw, bouncing over pebbles on the recently dug-up road, took us to a distance worth 5 rupees; that is, up to the next crossroads where the Janata Hotel owned by Ramchandra Gwala stood.

One hundred and thirty years old; rent: 130 rupees a night. The floor of the bathroom was reddened by the water of the Lohit (Brahmaputra); the corridors were dimly lit by red zero-watt bulbs; the doors were a faded red; and dust poured down from the ventilators until midnight. The mosquito nets had holes in them, and the greasy mattresses crawled with cockroaches. Cardboard had taken the place of glass on the windows and on every door were heavy handlelocks made of blackened brass. This elderly hotel *had* to find grandchildren-guests like us. Underneath our room, outside, was the city bus stand, the first after the railway station. Two voices would come through clearly in the din—

'Ulubari, Adabari, Panjabari, Dispur…'
'Ulubari, Adabari, Panjabari, Dispur…'

The other voice was that of a teenager who would endlessly repeat in a reedy voice: 'Come, eat; come, eat; come, eat…' After having steadily shouted for four hours on an empty stomach, the boy would receive food and 20 rupees as wages. After all the sounds ceased at night, religious chanting from the nearby naamghar would be clearly audible, the thin, high voices of children entwined among those of other singers. These were the collective prayers of a poverty-stricken people, desperate for relief in that unceasing terror.

In the night we went out to ask after the Brahmaputra. Biharis from remote districts of the state had camped on the deserted footpaths on the riverbank and were cooking meals over makeshift stoves put together with bricks. These people hadn't managed to board the trains travelling to their des because they had been overcrowded. Terror unleashed by the massacres, the helplessness of migration, and indignation flickered in the red of the fires burning under aluminum pots in these dark corners of the city. In contrast to the misery of these migrants suddenly made homeless, steamers past their prime stood moored on the Brahmaputra and the brightly lit restaurants upon them shimmered late into the night. These restaurants, which were being run on vessels that had been auctioned off by the government, still bore the same old names—Fairy Queen, Jalpari, Dolphin.

That night, there was both haze and fog. The whole city had been dug up. Many flyovers and streets were being constructed. The crowd of people and vehicles appeared to wobble through the refraction of the fog. Under bright, newly installed sodium lights, rickshaw-pullers were bouncing along over loose pebbles, flickering wick-lamps attached to their handlebars. They were still diligently observing a directive issued in the British era. From the state of the footpaths, it seemed as if elections loomed large. In Assam, development and massacres take place hand in hand before each election. Development for the middle classes of the cities and massacres to polarize the rural Assamese are the tried-and-tested formulae which take people into polling booths.

A small, prosperous Rajasthan thrives in the heart of Fancy Bazaar and Pan Bazaar, the commercial centres of the city; its religious icons are Vitthalji and Rani Sati who are duly covered in gauzy fabric and installed in small marble temples. Marwari hotels which serve onion- and garlic-less food, jalebis, phuchkas and the vehicles of the latest models stuffed into the narrow lanes proclaim other glories. The elderly MLA (Member of the Legislative Assembly) of the CPI (Communist Party of India), Hemant Das, had once explained to me in his inimitable style how more than 100 per cent of the wholesale trade in Assam is in the hands of Marwaris. The Assamese are merely consumers, he had said. Goods were being loaded and unloaded from hundreds of trucks in the godowns behind the bazaar. All the porters were either purabiyas—from eastern Uttar Pradesh and western Bihar in the Hindi belt—or Muslims from Mymensingh in Bangladesh. I didn't go there because of an old fear. In every such lane of every big city, I come across these porters, people I know from my village, district and nearby districts—people who had once been self-sufficient farmers. I can't face them, nor can they face me. Similar, familiar, saddening stories of migration and distress are to be found everywhere.

Guwahati, for an age, has been the biggest centre of trade for the Northeast. There are many ancient shops in the city which stock only salt, battery-operated torches and lanterns. Tribals from far-flung and remote jungles come in caravans to buy these goods. The USP of these stores is that they have arrangements for regular customers to stay in their backyards. The pig-market here is a remarkable place where the language of trade is Punjabi and Bhojpuri because most of the pigs come from Punjab and Bihar.

On reading the newspapers, it became clear that things were much worse than we had anticipated on the train. The Northeast is outside the circle of concern for Delhi-based media. In fact, it has been blacked out. The situation here was much more complicated and fearsome than even in Kashmir. In Duliajan and Kakojan, on 22 October, sixteen Hindi-speakers had been murdered; in Nalbari, on 27 October, ten; in Barpeta, on 8 November, ten; in Betawar, on 16 November, eight; in Nalbari, on 25 November, four; and in Bongaigaon, ten Hindi-speakers had been killed on 30 November. Apart from these, at least seven murders had happened in remote areas which had not been reported. A core group comprising representatives of the Army, the Home Ministry and the Assam Police were holding a meeting in which Joint Secretary N.R. Pillai from Delhi was representing Lal Krishna Advani, the home minister.

Tired of the excess of rubbery local fish and plain rice, we found an eatery near the Nepali Mandir which served maida parathas and chickpea chholey. And, afterwards, 'malai sumsum' for a sweet dish. Later, this same 'malai sumsum' was to become a symbol of good luck for us. The Assamese language does not possess the phonetic sound 'ch'. Thus cha, tea, becomes 'sa'. There's also an upper caste, the Sutiya, whose name is actually spelt 'Chutiya' in English.

We were eating there one afternoon. News was being broadcast on the television in front of us. After a Bihari man was murdered, his head had been crushed with a large stone. The man's brains lay spilled on the screen of the colour television two-and-a-half feet from where we were eating. I could feel the froth rise inside my stomach. Shashwat scolded me, 'There fucker, now look at a crushed head. We've come here to conduct journalism. Everywhere one looks there's a corpse, and not a single man will open his mouth to talk. Wouldn't it have been better to have stayed at home quietly? We would have heard the things Father would have to say but at least one could have eaten in peace.'

'Yaar, you're complaining like a poverty-stricken father who gave in to his son's demands and is regretting it.' I teased him, hoping to be distracted from my urge to throw up.

His anger was justified. The socialist from Lucknow, Girish Pandey, had given us the address of another supposedly helpful socialist leader, but the man had died four years earlier. Rambahadur Rai, the journalist, had given us details for three reporters: two were dead, the third had retired and found religion. The editor of the Lucknow edition of the *Pioneer*, Uday Sinha, had written an introduction to a newspaper-owner but, at our very first meeting, the man ranted: 'What does Sinha know other than to chew paan? He has destroyed our paper.' Prabhash Joshi had given us an address for Ravindra Bhai, a disciple of Vinoba Bhave, of the Anchalik Gramdan Sangh, but he was nowhere to be found. Sandeep Kshitij had given us film director Jahnu Barua's number but he was then in Kolkata.

There was one more thing. On the very first day I had categorically refused to garland my neck with Shashwat's camera—a simple contraption of the sort gifted to children on birthdays. I have an old dislike of looking like a pompous tourist. Shashwat had bought the camera to take the last pictures of his ancestral house in Sultanpur before it was to be sold off.

~

We now had to begin our journalism. After having slept for a year in depression, I was set to cover militancy in the Northeast. I had procured a fake ID from an irregularly published eight-page weekly that was involved in everything other than journalism in which I was described as the Delhi bureau chief. I had been given this card by a boy working in the weekly, duly rubber-stamped, without the owner's knowledge. Due to a typing error, my birthday had been marked the correct date, but exactly a century earlier. As 'identifying mark', it was written, in incorrect spelling, that I had a scar inside my left eye. The card had been laminated. Attempts to correct the mistakes would have left it tattered. I had never paid attention to these things earlier. Shashwat didn't have even this card. We first decided to call the numbers appearing alongside the printlines of local newspapers and speak to journalists in Guwahati to decide the course of our journalistic canoe in a river of blood.

Our first meeting was with the editor Ajit Bhuyan, who, until a few days ago, had been incarcerated on TADA (Terrorist and Disruptive Activities [Preventive]) charges for allegedly aiding the ULFA and who was then busy establishing a brand-new newspaper, *Aaji*. A reporter working for a television channel reporter had told us about Bhuyan—who was a good-looking, personable man—that Matang Sinh, member of the Rajya Sabha, had invested his black money in Bhuyan's venture. But the dusty Rajgarh Link Road, suffused with the stink of rotting water, on which Bhuyan's office was situated presented another picture altogether. Bhuyan met us with his own set of complaints: 'The Prafulla Kumar Mahanta government is putting roadblocks in the loan-giving process. I haven't received an electricity connection and a generator is being used to bring out the newspaper.'

I heard Ajit Bhuyan's name invoked in a poem being broadcast from a loudspeaker one-and-a-half months later, after the SULFA (Surrendered United Liberation Front of Assam) began raiding houses belonging to militants in joint operations with the police. That midnight, a teenaged Bengali poet sang at an artists' gathering which had been organized near the Dighali Pukhuri to protest the massacres and the terror: 'We will become Ajit Bhuyan, we will become Parag Das.' The writer, Parag Das, who was murdered by the SULFA, has the status of a martyr in Assam. Ajit Bhuyan, who was once Parag Das's friend, was unwilling to say anything about the government's attitude towards the militants and land into fresh trouble. He had many old problems.

~

The new Joint Task Force formed to tackle terrorism was holding a press conference at the Army headquarters in Lalmati. We reached the Brahmaputra Hotel that morning. The sofas in the lounge of the hotel and the streets outside it were meeting places for local reporters because every VIP visiting from Delhi would stay there. From there, we hitched a ride in a dilapidated jeep belonging to the state information department and reached the Army headquarters where rows of chairs, covered with starched, dazzlingly white fabric, stood in a sprawling lawn. Army officers in olive-green uniforms and policemen in khaki were chanting 'ISI-ISI' in a rhythmic litany. Colonel Mahesh Vij of the GOC Corps was explaining: 'It is because of our friendly attitude towards citizens that our killing capacity has increased by almost one hundred per cent. In the last three years, in comparison to earlier years, we have eliminated almost two times the number of terrorists and have forced about 2,000 to surrender.'

'Dur kela!' An Assamese reporter, to whom I had been introduced just two hours earlier, said to me, 'One man surrenders four times for government loans. If you don't believe, I take you to tailor from whom Army officers get ULFA uniforms stitched for surrendering militants.'

Home Secretary Pillai, who had flown in from Delhi, was explaining how the ULFA, fearful of the success of the Joint Task Force, was going after soft targets so that they could register their presence in Assam. Now the ULFA has no ideology, he said, and it has become a purely terrorist organization. A question which had long been simmering inside me spilled out even before Mr Pillai could complete his statement: 'If the ULFA must find soft targets, why are they not killing the Bangladeshi interlopers who had prompted the agitation in Assam in the first place... After all, it was the failure of the government to send back Bangladeshi migrants which had pushed some discontented boys of the Asom Gana Parishad into forming the ULFA... But here, it is the citizens of the country who are being murdered.' A sly smirk began to play on the faces of all the people present, as if I had said something ridiculous, something which even children knew about.

'And you are?' When Pillai asked me this question instead of replying to mine, my legs quaked. If he demanded my proof of identity, I would be exposed. Gathering courage, I said a little too loudly, 'I'm from Delhi.' It was the director-general of the Assam Police, H.K. Deka, who began a reply, 'Because ULFA has gone over completely into ISI's hands. *You* report every day that they have their headquarters in Dhaka. That arms for the ULFA arrive at the Cox Bazaar Port. That Baruah and other leaders of ULFA own malls and business complexes in Dhaka. That they also have satellite phones from Pakistan. Try and recollect the headlines of your own newspapers; you will understand everything.'

My entire attention was hooked not by the content of the director-general's reply, but by the way in which he pronounced English words. He was a poet of renown but, at that moment, he was speaking like a supercop from a Hollywood crime thriller. I thought of the sahuain's daughters from the train, that family from Moreh. I felt the girls and the director-general had innovated language in similar ways—the former for survival and the latter for the sake of his job. People were being murdered all around; militants were striking at will, at times and places of their choosing. The Army and the police had mastered the art of media-managing the ceremonies marking fake encounters and surrenders, all of which were sorely burdened by the excessively long and flowery speeches made by politicians. In such a situation, words were ammunition that were more valuable than bullets and kept alive the illusion that much was being done to contain the militancy.

An old bespectacled reporter, sniffing for a story within the four walls of media-management, asked: 'Is the militancy simply a law-and-order problem or does a state of war with Delhi exist?'

'You tell us. We want to know what you think too.' The lieutenant-general stalled the question.

A jaded cameraman was grumbling at the back of the room, 'Bamboozled us with one stale pastry and black tea—so much hot air for so little.'

I was also disappointed. I had thought that we would get proper food at least at the Army Headquarters but the gamble hadn't paid off.

Afterwards, we met numerous gentlefolk and asked all of them why these Hindi-speakers—labourers, agrarian workers, milkmen—were being killed. What these generals, officers and intellectuals couldn't tell me, I heard later in the sad monologue of an Assamese fisherman and in the gibberish of a Bihari drunk.

~

The corridors of the Janata Hotel were dark and damp. Clothes spread out on the balconies to dry would keep reeking. On those cold winter days the roof of the hotel had small patches of sunlight but it also carried a mountain of empty alcohol bottles and heaps of rotting trash. On days when we couldn't find the guides—meaning, intellectuals—to describe to us the corpse-filled forts of the militants, I would take my sleeping bag and make my way to the river. I would lie topless, sunbathing on the deck of a government steamer long past its sell-by date and, putting together letters of the Assamese alphabet, try to read the paper and fall off into a sleep.

Shashwat was trying to set up a meeting with the then governor of Assam, retired lieutenant-general S.K. Sinha. During those days the governor was busy telling people that they should combat militants with sticks, batons and stones. The old general's martial spirit was clearly evident, even in the media. General Sinha—originally from Bihar—was married to the sister of a nephew of Babu Ganpat Sahay—who was ex-MP (Member of Parliament) from Sultanpur, a famous lawyer, as well as Shashwat's grandfather. Shashwat first wanted to meet Her Highness Aunt. Thereafter His Excellency Uncle would automatically himself meet us and we would get governmental support for our travels, even in that violence. This would be especially important in the plateaus of Upper Assam, where the ULFA maintained its bases, and where, we had been told by intellectuals, it was unadvisable to travel without police protection. In those areas, they also said, reporters from Delhi were looked upon as agents working for Army intelligence organizations.

Shashwat had kept his intended appointment with Her

Highness Aunt secret from me. Passing by the Guwahati Club, we would regularly stop to eat pakoras at a shop run by a Bihari woman. One day, I read to her the governor's appeal from a newspaper. The old woman became furious and started to curse, 'A chutiya has come for a lattgub'nor, Bhaiya! Ram Ram! He says we should confront the ULFA with lumps of clay.' Shashwat knew what I thought of the governor. He must have deduced that if I was present at the meeting with his uncle, things could go very wrong.

At the river was a new celestial world. This wasn't a she-river, but a deep, mighty he-river of winter. The pillar which indicated the height of the waters in the flood season stood naked and ignored. The tiny Umananda Mandir island would keep gazing at the Kamakhya Mandir hills all day and nodding its head at them. The lighthouse built to guide steamers on the river would uselessly switch on and off even in broad daylight. As soon as dusk fell, fantasies would bubble up inside me. In the haze of winter, the dismembered arms, the gigantic buttocks, the eroding shoulders, the staring eyes of a clay goddess cast upon the riverbank—half-woman, half-straw—would combine and become languorous women stretched out on the shore. And, before I could know it, the goddess would rattle all the weapons she carried in her eight arms and warn me, the sinner who had cast a rapacious eye upon his own mother.

In the mornings, a procession of people would arrive, going to work or to buy things, on steamers from the far side of the river. The shops set up on the riverbank would shake off their lethargy and become alert. In the evening those same people would travel back to the far side on the steamers along with their bicycles, carrying vegetables, pigeons and articles of daily use. The afternoons would be uncrowded and peaceful. The children playing cricket on the shining expanse of sand of the far bank would seem to twinkle and the restaurants on the steamers would doze in the sun.

On one such afternoon, I wrote in my diary:

There is a strange pleasure in lying on the deck of this desolate, rundown steamer on the Brahmaputra, listening to the songs broadcast on a faraway radio, faint at times, clear at others. A fountain of notes bursts forth, vanishes among the raucous cawing of crows circling the river bank, and surfaces elsewhere. This pleasure cannot be found in any musical soiree. At the soiree there is waiting, the grammar of music, and heaps of ennui. Here, music has dissolved into the very waves of the river and the steamers sway to its rhythm. In the distance, a motorboat engine whirs. A slim boat is whizzing, and boring its way into the sun. The water, the hills and the horizon are all enveloped in a blue haze. A hawk hunts fish in the river. Crows follow the hawk; helpless dependents who caw meekly: 'Spare some for us, too, master, spare some…' Oleanders floating on the surface of the water—offerings at a puja—are smouldering in the sun's glow. Waterfowl have gathered on a floating log and chatter away in a conference.

These creaking boats, with their beds, utensils and oars, represent a world about whose pleasures and pains we know nothing. Just as we don't know how the Brahmaputra becomes a highway for ULFA and Bodo militants at night. An old shopkeeper on the ghat tells a tourist that the Hindus here don't eat chicken but pigeon-meat. This is an everyday task for the man. He makes this pronouncement like he is revealing a mystical secret about religion and, afterwards, he sighs a deep breath of satisfaction.

'A slim boat is whizzing, and boring its way into the sun.' Hunh! What a fake description of that scene this was. Here was no brave oarsman challenging the heat of the sun. These were all just poor fishermen who were rapidly reeling in their nets in the falling dusk. The procurers for the hotels on the riverbank were all shouting and cursing them to hurry up so that they would receive their supplies on time.

One day, Duloo Bharali roused me from the crows-and-radio orchestra and took me with a great deal of affection to see his makeshift boat. After having used the wooden oars from his old boat to cook local fish, he had had a new diesel engine installed. River water sucked up through a pipe would keep the engine cool and flow back into the river from the other side. Sitting on the edge of the boat, he would use a long pole to determine the direction of its travel. To increase or decrease speed he would manipulate the nozzle-pin of the engine with a short stick. He had spent a total of 17,000 rupees to modify his boat and charged me—after the bonus of a Coca-Cola smile, with tamul-corroded gums—nothing for the ride. He offered me a soothsayer's self-caution along with everything else: 'If I take money from younger brother, leprosy will strike me.'

This was perfect. Now I could do as I pleased—sleep all day on the deck of the steamer in the warmth of the winter sun, or ferry people from one shore to the other as an apprentice to Duloo-da. One day, as we waited mid-river for a Bihari family who had gone to the Umananda Mandir for one last darshan before returning to their des, Begusarai, Duloo-da said to himself in Assamese, in a lost voice, 'How are the ULFA brave? They are killing the poor.'

According to Duloo-da, the SULFA, after taking money from the government, would soon target houses belonging to ULFA leaders. ULFA commander Paresh Baruah's house had been attacked only a few days earlier when his mother Miliki Baruah had been home alone. She had pleaded with the bombers to talk some sense into her son. After the attack on ULFA chairman Arabinda Rajkhowa's house, his father, who had been a freedom fighter, had grieved that the service he had offered the country had gone in vain. At the time of the attack, Rajkhowa's sister had appeared for an examination for the post of police inspector. Duloo-da was unwilling to believe at any cost that the ULFA would drive the Biharis out from Assam merely in exchange for money and arms from the ISI. He shouted over the roar of the engine, 'There will be elections in the coming year. There's politics in these murders. Everything has to do with the elections, Bhaiti. That party which supports the kicking out of the Biharis will have the support of all the Muslims, whether citizens or outsiders. There are forty constituencies where Muslims are present in decisive numbers.' One among them was Nagaon, Chief Minister Prafulla Kumar Mahanta's constituency, where the Nellie massacre had taken place during Indira Gandhi's tenure as prime minister.

At that time, a team of four MPs sent to Assam by Bangaru Laxman, national president of the ruling party, BJP—the same Bangaru of the *Tehelka* sting-operation fame—was travelling in the state. These MPs had reported that both the Congress and the Asom Gana Parishad counted Muslims as their votebank and were therefore helping the ULFA. Both these parties wanted the BJP's Hindi-language-speaking voter base to flee the state before the upcoming elections. Since the AGP supporting Vajpayee's ruling alliance at the Centre, it was being given a long leash. This was being done by announcing that the BJP and the AGP were jointly asking for the Illegal Migrants (Determination by Tribunal) Act, 1983, to be revisited but the Congress was unwilling to consider it. The Bangladeshis are traditionally supporters of the Congress. In fact, by raising violence against Biharis to a fever pitch, the Congress wanted to have President's Rule imposed in the state so that it could use its old and loyal bureaucratic machinery to come back to power.

Duloo-da's finger on the pulse of Assam was as sure as his hand was on the bamboo stick with which he pressed the engine nozzle to control the speed of his boat.

It was then that the real political drama began at the chief minister's residence after the killings in Sadiya. On 7 December, militants had stopped a truck full of Bihari labourers in the Kukurmara jungle between Tinsukia and Arunachal Pradesh, stood them in a line, asked them for their names and addresses and shot them all down. Thirty men died. Their corpses lay rotting for two days. So great was the terror that no journalist could visit the spot. The first journalist to reach was a Naga girl, Bano Haralu, who went with the health minister of Assam in his cavalcade on the third day.

Chief Minister Prafulla Kumar Mahanta had invited reporters to his residence and was playing them a video cassette. An old man who seemed mentally disturbed was on screen, claiming he was once a party-worker for the Congress. The man then raised his hands and wailed to god that these murders were being carried out by the Congress through the ULFA so that Bangladeshi immigrants would find a place in Assam and the Congress could secure the immigrant vote. These massacres have broken my heart, the old man would say, and I am resigning from my post. Switching off the television, Mahanta would declare: 'So *that* is the truth. The Congress wants to dismiss my government and impose President's Rule.'

On the contrary, Mahanta wasn't at all worried about President's Rule being imposed. He was very close to the governor, Lieutenant General S.K. Sinha, and Sinha would frequently address the chief minister as 'Prafulla Kumar, my son,' even on public forums.

The state Congress president and chief-minister-in-waiting, Tarun Gogoi, was playing a video cassette of his own. He would tell the journalists gathered to mooch dinner at his house that the old man in the video was an AGP man. In return for calling himself a party-worker for the Congress, the government had built him a pukka house. That's the magic of our party, he would say, you take our name and a pukka house will stand in the place of a hovel.

Far more farsighted than these parties and leaders, smearing blame for the massacres on each others' foreheads and trying to draw voters into their respective camps, was a bedraggled drunk I would frequently see around midnight on the streets near Cotton College, jerking and weaving along as if he were a bird controlled by invisible strings. With an unlikely balance and clear-sightedness, achieved between exuberance, fear and plain drunkenness, he had foreseen events which would occur many years later. That night, he was weeping like a child. He had a rusted, handleless razor in hand which he would brandish now and then with quick movements. Who could tell how many necks he had slit by the time I met him. His dust-covered beard gleamed with tears as he screamed in a cracking voice: 'Who says Assamese originally from here? They migrated from Burma. When we kick them out of Patna Medical College, what will happen?'

His prediction shook me. I offered him my cigarette and, to start a conversation, asked, 'Who is kicking whom out, Bhaiya?'

He slapped the cigarette out of my hand and shouted, 'No one can kick out anyone. All will cut each other dead. Asomiya says first Bengali oppressed and now Bihari oppress. Bodo says Asomiya oppress. Same way Rabha speaks against Bodo, Miri against Rabha, Tiwa against Miri, and Dimasa speaks against Tiwa. Everyone ready to fight each other. Who can kick anyone out like this?'

Many months later, I understood that this was a true picture of the struggles between the many nationalities and tribal cultures of the Northeast. Every prominent tribal community has its own militant organization fighting for a separate land and a literary organization working to develop its own script. The Hmar community includes 30,000 individuals but even they are fighting against the colonial attitude of the governments of Assam and Delhi.

According to the authorities, there aren't enough of them to even make up a district.

That question which I couldn't pose to any Bihari fleeing from Assam, I asked the drunk: 'But why are the Biharis being kicked out?'

The man strenuously chased the cigarette being blown about by the wind and caught it. He took a deep drag and began patiently, 'Asomiya man is a tender man. He will play flute, sing song, do theatre, wear clean gamcha and chew tamul and gossip all day but he will not go to field and get hand dirty. He want to do only government job and eat rice. He won't farm. The Biharis worked hard and built houses, shops and farms. Asomiya think these damnfool people will occupy all of Assam and turn into Bihar. The Mymensinghi from Bangladesh too is a farmer from birth, like the Bihari. When the leaders were shouting that the Mymensinghi Muslims had to be kicked out, Asomiya were settling them on their farms. They need labour. Bangladeshis still enter through Tripura, giving soldier at border forty rupees but now land is less people more. So everywhere is violence.'

Professor Amalendu Guha, considered an eccentric sort of an intellectual, had tried to explain something similar in English in a cultured way to a gathering of intellectuals in a seminar. This seminar, on the 'Constitutional Safeguards of the Assamese People', had been held on 9 December in the Institute of Bank Management in Khanapara. Other intellectuals, experts in the ways of seminars, had prevented him from putting his views forward. All he could manage to say was: 'This, possibly, is not an Assamese versus Other Cultures phenomena. No one realizes that this battle is being fought over who has the right to our limited resources, a battle in which culture is being used as the chief weapon. It is not the culture of Assam which is under threat but, rather, its politics and its economy.' Culture has been an aching wound in Assam for hundreds of years. Every sort of manoeuvering has been disguised under the garb of culture. This seminar had been organized with funding from Delhi by an NGO, the Northeast Foundation.

The office in-charge of the Northeast Foundation was Pikumani Dutta, a romantic revolutionary who had just left the Communist Party to see if he could find a political future in the NGO. Like the hero of the Cuban revolution Che Guevara, Dutta always wore a beret with a red star on it. From the contexts of his conversations, one would think the man lived in a camp in some jungle and not in the city of Guwahati. I spent many evenings with Dutta. One evening he said, 'The ULFA has completely degraded. The Army, which once used to find Marxist literature in ULFA bunkers, now finds pictures of heroines from Hindi movies, the novels of Ranjit Barua, condoms and empty liquor bottles.' Another day he took a look at my identity card and declared that I was an agent working for the Army intelligence masquerading as a reporter.

~

As residents of the Janata Hotel, we were beginning to experience the boundaries of gentility. There was a need to meet a member of the ULFA so that we could understand—without a mediator—if the ULFA was actually being directed by the ISI, as well as the organization's attitude towards the killing of Hindi-speakers. I spoke to Mohanan Dada-aan. He was a born reporter. He had landed up in Assam from Kerala to find a job in a newspaper and was working for an electronic-media channel at the time. He was considered quite a wheeler-dealer in journalistic circles, even though he was from distant south India. He advised: 'The ULFA website is up and running. Go chat online with Paresh Baruah. But you can't meet them. When those people want to meet you, you will be picked up from wherever you are staying. And then you can have your meeting.'

The cadre of the ULFA and its media-manager were in town. What we didn't know was how to meet them. The ways of checking up on the credibility of a reporter from out of town were so uncertain and secret that one could not tell anything in advance.

One evening, we set out to meet Bhrigu Kumar Phukan—once considered the think tank of the Assam Revolution and number two in Prafulla Kumar Mahanta's government—but reached a neighbourhood carom club instead. There we met the 'Enigma Commander' of the ULFA—a post unique to that organization—Ramen Nath. Nath had surrendered a month earlier. Two men from the Assam Police were standing at the entrance to the club and, outside, three or four SULFA cadres were sitting in a government-issue Gypsy, wielding AK-47s. Ramen Nath was playing carom with his friends. From the atmosphere, it could be sensed how, rapidly, in a month's time, Ramen Nath had transformed from a guerilla fighter into a local hood.

I reproduced for him Duloo Bharali's question

verbatim: 'How brave is the ULFA that it targets poor people?' Ramen Nath replied simply, 'The ULFA can do anything now. It is being run not by the Assamese but by the Pathans of Jonwai [the land of the star and the sickle moon, Pakistan]. The organization's executive committee hasn't even met in two years. The leaders all run their businesses in Bangladesh. Now, the real work is spreading terror, extortion and running fake currency.'

Assured under the protection of the government, Nath was speaking in a balanced, frank manner. 'We went into the jungles for a sovereign Assam, after having read books, but when we saw that our leaders, under orders from the Pathans, were having even Asomiya people killed, we surrendered.'

'And what if the ULFA punishes you for turning traitor?'

'We're not Bihari or Bhutani that they will kill us so easily.' He pointed to the Gypsy standing outside. 'We don't wear bangles. It's not like our guns fire lemon candy.'

'Bhutani! Why will ULFA murder Bhutanis?'

Ramen Nath avoided my question then but the following January, petty traders from Bhutan were murdered in Lower Assam. These traders come each year to sell warm clothes; they had come that year too. The difference that year was that the Bhutanese royalty, under pressure from the Indian government, had passed a resolution in their Assembly that the ULFA camps within Bhutanese territory should be dismantled. By killing the traders, the ULFA was threatening the king of Bhutan that he should not pressurize them to dismantle their camps.

After this unexpected meeting, I sent my first story on militancy in the Northeast to Delhi, which was never published in any newspaper.

We had an agreement with the chief editor of a national daily that he would print our dispatches from the Northeast. That day I faxed my article six times and ran up a bill of 260 rupees. By the time a clear, readable copy went through, the chief editor had left for the day and there was no one left in office to take a call on whether to publish the article or not. What had actually happened was this: The chief editor had been so excited by our proposal of travel-reportage that he had promised us 2,500 rupees per story but hadn't been able to manage to get even 500 rupees sanctioned by his newspaper's accounts department.

The chief editor said to us later that we didn't possess the skill required to market our work. The truth was that his newspaper had no interest in carrying stories of militancy in the Northeast. In those days they were busy setting up regional editions to tap the emerging Hindi-language revenue markets of UP and Bihar. The chief editor in question was *Hindustan*'s Ajay Upadhyay, who later gave me a job in the newspaper but who couldn't get my reports published then. We were discouraged by this failure and were talking to and wooing various other editors in Delhi when Mohanan Dada-aan invited us to Shillong. His crew was visiting the dorbar of the tribal king of Shillong to cover it.

It was Shashwat who had christened the man Mohanan Dada-aan on our first meeting. Every time Mohanan was asked something, he would reply in the pinched tone of a startled bird: 'Aan!' In the South Indian way of speaking, it is not uncommon for the syllable 'ha' to drop away, and for 'hamara' to become 'amara', but this 'aan' in place of 'haan' was something else. What's more, Mohanan Dada's current refrain when we met him was 'Balls', perhaps under the influence of an English film or novel. He would exclaim at everything: 'Balls!' Mohanan hears and thinks with his testicles, some of his friends had begun to say. We understood this complicated process in this way: someone takes Mohanan Dada's name, and the words hit his balls. Since the testicles are excruciatingly sensitive, it is only natural that they hurt like hell, and an 'aan' escapes his lips, like the anguished squawk of a lapwing.

~

Soon after Jorabat on the National Highway, small earthen hillocks which were covered with bamboo groves, and banana and pineapple plantations, heaved into sight. Nepali women, sitting in front of small bamboo houses on the roadside were openly baring their breasts and suckling babies. The oranges which tribal men and women had brought from their villages in tall bamboo baskets were being sold dirt-cheap. At first glance, it seemed as if security was very tight since buses coming from Meghalaya—which shares an extended border with Bangladesh—were being stopped and thoroughly checked. But, on closer scrutiny, it became clear that the people who were being taken off the buses for show were simply catching another bus or taxi and continuing their journey.

En route, we came upon the beautiful, calm and massive Umiam Lake on whose shore a lone boy was standing, trying to flag down cars so he could sell the 7-kilogramme carp he had hanging at the end of a thin cord. As we ascended the slope up to the lake, the cold assaulted us. All at once, stands of old pine trees took the place of bamboo, pineapple and banana in the scenery that was flashing past before our eyes. From the skyline, one felt that the British had built this place—which was dear to them—in the image of a European city from the Victorian era.

On reaching the syiem's house, we found that the royal audience had already gathered three days earlier at Motphran Chowk. This audience was being held again for the benefit of television channels. The Khasi king, in traditional headgear, adorned with pearls and shells, and carrying his ancestral sword, munched on potato chips and sipped Coke as he read out from a handout written in English: 'Consensus is being formed among all the twenty-five kingdoms of Meghalaya that the Indian government must amend the Constitution to reinstate the monarchical system here, for this system has, in every way, proved better than the corrupt and unjust democracy currently in place.'

The city of Shillong falls within the boundaries of the ancient Hima Mylliem kingdom controlled by its syiem, Loborious Manik Syiem. The king's audience which had gathered three days earlier at Motphran Chowk had come together for the first time in seventy years and the Khasis had all gathered in their traditional costumes. The drums and yodels of war had played; animal sacrifices had been made. Five thousand representatives of the traditional panchayats from the surrounding hills had all raised their hands and implored the king to protect the old ways, and to initiate a struggle so that the Khasi kingdoms would receive Constitutional sanction. But, today, chickens were being sacrificed for lunch for reporters from Guwahati and they were being served foreign liquor instead of traditional drinks. It was strange—women are traditionally the heads of Khasi families, but not one was to be found here.

One of the reporters enjoying the feast asked, 'Raja saheb, will you support the Jaintias and the Garos if they demand their old kingdoms back?' This simple-seeming question was a joke. For the king doubled over laughing. Then he said, 'The Garos won't demand their own kingdom because so many Bangladeshis have settled in their territories that they are themselves in a minority there. They wouldn't want a king from Mymensingh.'

An anti-New Delhi agitation was shaking things up in Shillong. The effect of the agitation on a people—sick of the horrific corruption of the political class, the constant shifting of party allegiances by leaders and the violence perpetrated by the militants—could be clearly observed. The push for the reinstatement of the monarchy had the support of the banned organization, the Hynniewtrep National Liberation Council (HNLC), as well. It seemed as if the threadbare garments, headgear and rusty swords were seeing the light of day in ages. That week, at another assembly in the ancient kingdom of Kheem, the largest in Meghalaya, the king Balajik Singh Syiem has called for a political revolution to reinstate the traditional Khasi monarchical system. A smaller kingdom, Nongstoin, was also to hold its dorbar whose king, Syiem Sib Singh, in 1947, had refused to sign the document which would merge the kingdom with India, as part of a proposal made by Sardar Vallabhbhai Patel. Due to this refusal, the deputy king, U Wickliffe Syiem, spent his life in exile in East Pakistan (later, Bangladesh). The Khasi militants have given U Wickliffe Syiem the status of a martyr who died fighting for independence. When two kingdoms, Nongsiej and Rambrai, refused the merger, the deputy commissioner and the dominion agent of the British Empire, G.P. Jorman threatened the kingdoms until they agreed. It is a fact that during those days, when the most powerful kings were clamouring for refuge, these two tiny principalities agreed to merge with India only at the very end. Speeches were being made at the dorbars that India had forcibly taken over the Khasi kingdoms.

The syiems of the smaller kingdoms were explaining to their people that, on 15 January 1947, an agreement was struck between Akbar Haideri, then the governor of Assam, and the Khasi kingdoms that barring defence, currency and foreign policy, every other matter would be decided upon by the Khasis, and their syiems, themselves. Later, however, these kingdoms were tricked into being included in the Sixth Schedule of the Constitution and autonomous councils were set up in the Khasi, Garo and Jaintia districts ostensibly to run the administration along traditional lines. Thus the syiems had been reduced to kings in name only. The councils would use them like pawns and install and remove them at will.

To gain a foothold in the Lok Sabha elections of 1998, the BJP had promised that it would honour the Akbar Haideri treaty in its original form. In the following elections, the Garo leader P.A. Sangma, former Speaker of the Lok Sabha, fighting for his political survival, contested on the National Congress ticket, under the symbol of the 'watch', and promised the Jaintia people that he would amend the Indian Constitution to reinstate monarchy. The National Commission to Review the Working of the Constitution was set up around that time and the issue received the oxygen it so desperately needed.

The autonomous councils which had been set up to safeguard traditional laws and customs and traditional structures had become rapidly bureaucratized. In imitation of ministers and MLAs, these organizations were rife with scheming and with dynastic politics. These autonomous councils, which hold the right to install or remove the syiems, were the nurseries for the new leaders of Meghalaya, all of whom were masters at hopping parties. Their greatest weapon was the United Khasi-Jaintia Hills Autonomous District (Appointment and Succession of Chiefs and Headmen) Act, 1959. If a king was not to their liking, they would simply remove him. According to the councils, most kings are drunk and corrupt. If they were to receive constitutional sanction, they say, the kings would become lords who don't listen to anyone's counsel. They are forever ready to sell their lands to non-tribals. And there is always the possibility of corruption in the ways in which these illiterate landlords collect and account for tax.

The result of this conflict is that, in contemporary Meghalaya, three laws—administered by traditional structures, the Indian government, and the autonomous councils—run together, and citizens hang suspended from this spiderweb. For instance, the police cannot enter localities in the state capital Shillong without the express permission of the traditional chiefs. This is their biggest impediment in battling militancy.

Our teeth chattered in the cold wind even though the sunlight fell warmly upon us as we stood outside the king's house. Heavily laden orange trees stood in front of those houses which had even the smallest strip of a lawn.

Beautiful, clear-complexioned girls ran shops with the assurance that springs from owning your business. The self-confidence engendered by being raised in a matrilineal society was upon their faces. In Khasi folktales, the sun is feminine and the moon masculine. And, certainly, Khasi men are visible only in the light of their womenfolk. Property is handed down to the youngest daughter of the household—the 'ka kuddu'. If the men must take a bank loan, it is the women's guarantee which stands valid. But these beautiful girls were all right only until they smiled; the moment they did, a wave of fear would begin to swell in my heart. For most women had teeth—worn down after a lifetime of chewing kwai (the tamul in Meghalaya)—fitted into gums that would open like red saws. The beautiful faces which bore those teeth would remind me of the villainesses of Puranic stories.

After meeting the king, it was necessary to meet the new king, i.e. the chief minister, E.K. Mawlong, so that he could be asked for his government's views on the reinstatement of the monarchical system. His home minister, T.H. Rangad, had attended the Hima Mylliem dorbar and publicly demonstrated his fealty to the old king. The chief minister was in a Cabinet meeting and we had to return that evening. Trying to figure out an effective way to meet, we followed some leads and landed up in the office of the English newspaper *Meghalaya Guardian* where we met Frank, an extremely humble dipsomaniac reporter. Frank's elder brother, a minister, was inside attending the Cabinet meeting. Frank made a quick call and scheduled an interview. This was the first time I had seen a chief minister who called the press into a Cabinet meeting. In the Northeast, political leaders aren't as feudally stuffy and pompous as their counterparts from the Hindi belt are. They are still easily accessible.

Mawlong said guardedly that he accepted the existence of traditional kings and institutions and had never interfered in their workings. According to Home Minister Rangad, he had attended the dorbar not as a minister but in his position as the chief of his community.

Returning to Guwahati at night, the jeep we were travelling in broke down 5 kilometres before Nongpoh. The jeep had been crawling downhill for about 10 kilometres like a snail, spewing smoke, but most of us were excitedly chattering in an advanced state of drunkenness and we noticed it late. As active as the militants in Assam and Meghalaya were, the imaginations of the scared drivers plying the road were a thousand times more so; there was no chance that a bunch of eight or nine young men, laden with heavy bags, cameras and camera-stands, would receive a lift from any passing vehicle.

Even at midnight, pineapples, oranges and bananas were available at roadside shops. Drivers were eating at a few dhabas. They held the hands of the teenaged Nepali waitresses by way of placing their orders and a pinch on their cheeks was their mid-meal break. The way these girls were bubblingly cheerful, clad only in a T-shirt and a wraparound even in that freezing weather, excited one enough to think of the possibility that they were something more. As I was trying to improve my acquaintance with one of the girls, Mohanan Dada-aan sobered enough to shout at me. He dragged me out of the dhaba. 'These people will be provoked by outsiders.'

'The Nepalis are themselves outsiders, how will they be provoked by outsiders?'

'My dear, you see only Nepali chicks. I am talking about the local drivers.'

There was no option but to shoulder our loads and walk in the darkness. The pale moon shining over the deep green of the hillsides seemed intriguing. Only the topmost leaves of the banana, coconut, areca-nut and bamboo trees which made up the jungle received a silver glow from the moon. The bottom half remained shrouded in deep darkness. The effect of the moonlight was unnatural. One which with its mystery was enough to help us transcend the hardship of the steepest, most heart-stopping climbs. A taxi-driver in Nongpoh agreed, after great difficulty, to take us to Guwahati. It was sunrise by the time we reached.

~

A new journey began, one in tunnels of fear. Not an external journey but one within.

One morning, I saw my report printed in the *Purvanchal Prahari*, the sole significant Hindi-language newspaper of the Northeast even though I hadn't sent them anything I had written. It was true, of course, that I had had a meeting with the paper's editor, Satyanand Pathak. This paper belonged to G.L. Agarwala, a social worker and one of the biggest contractors of the forestry department of Assam, who ran the paper with his own unique swagger.

Sitting on the bank of the Dighali Pukhuri one afternoon I was trying to guess who would have submitted my article to the *Purvanchal Prahari* when Shashwat mumbled, 'The money has run out. There's nothing at all left now.'

I looked at him in astonishment. After having wandered about in an air laden with doubt and the stench of blood and corpses for so many days, I was afraid for the first time. I was having to make an effort to even inhale. The hotel expenses and the food bills had remained unpaid for many days. Fat bills had accumulated in the two PCOs from where we had made phones calls and sent faxes. Between us, we had perhaps 25 or 30 rupees. We had withdrawn more money from Shashwat's credit card than his limit allowed. His elder brother should have sent us money from Allahabad fifteen days earlier but this hadn't been possible. I wanted to shout, 'Why didn't you say so before? You've been cooking this alone all along, and you're telling me now when there isn't money enough to make any move at all!'

I said instead, 'So what? Ask your uncle, His Excellency the governor, for some. Have you figured out a way to meet him yet?'

Without demonstrating surprise at my knowledge of his secret plan, and after mumbling 'This is the limit!' numerous times, Shashwat spoke in the tone of a thorough gentleman: 'You're a proper cunt! Will I meet a relative after so many days and immediately ask him for money? What will he think? That I am destitute and beg for a living!'

After this, we never spoke about the governor again.

When we returned to the hotel at night, my eyes fell on the waiters in the dim red light of the corridor. Their arms were muscular. To travel to any state in the Northeast one must wait in Guwahati for a few hours for buses. It was because of travellers like these that this ancient and cheap establishment, the Janata Hotel, had flourished for one hundred and thirty years. Each room would be let out three or four times in a twenty-four-hour period. Each night, the bearers would hang bat-like to the ventilators of the rooms which had women in them. After every half an hour they could be seen huddled in the corridors, their heads together like members of an efficient sporting team, giving each other bulletins from the rooms they had been peeping into, and then swap rooms. It was this strenuous and hypnotic exercise which lasted until morning that had given them their burly arms.

Shashwat suffered a mild attack of low blood pressure, compounded by despair. He sat on the bed, alternately examining his palms. From experience, I knew this was the initial symptom. I went through our bags, and the pockets of all of our clothes, and then asked for the 13 rupees which Shashwat had with him. With that money I bought a quarter bottle of rum and began my ritual of drinking. It was decided that the following day the two rings belonging to Shashwat, and if needed, his mother's atehroo which was kept in his attaché, would be pawned in the local gold market to arrange for money. The atehroo is a Kashmiri ornament worn like an earring. We had pawned the same atehroo earlier at a shop which belonged to Ram Narayan Sahu, member of the Rajya Sabha from the Samajwadi Party.

Since we were strangers, no one in the gold-and-silver market of Fancy Bazaar was willing to pawn our ornament. And the ones who were, would not give us more than 500 or 1,000 rupees. Some, thinking us to be suspect, either toyed with us or ignored us. In the afternoon we began to bargain with gold merchants to sell the ornaments. The few merchants who expressed interest quoted 2,500-3,000 rupees when the rings alone were worth 15,000 rupees. A thought struck: Why not leave the ornaments as surety with the hotel-owner? Then another: If he guessed that we had both been completely cleaned out, he would simply deduct the amount due to him, return us the balance, and send us on our way. And then? We would have nothing left to pawn.

That evening, a Marwari gold-merchant advised that we should go to the back of the railway station, where the pig merchants were. Since they were purabiyas like us, they would help. We reached in a flash and found the pig merchants seated on beds—their surroundings lighted by small lamps—with herd upon porcine herd milling about them. They were all preparing to retire for the night inside mosquito nets even as the pigs set up a squealing and grunting in the final hours of their lives. The most number of pigs taken to the Northeast are from Punjab, Uttar Pradesh and Bihar. These people weren't pig-merchants but their servants who were staying there to take care of the animals. When we spoke to them, we found that they received food and a salary for their efforts. They were in no condition to pawn our rings. We came back to the hotel.

The following day, a boy manning a PCO took us to a gold-merchant, Bachcha Prasad Sonar, near the railway station. He, too, could do nothing. Prasad was a goldsmith who catered to women of the lower middle class and operated out of a small cubicle. He used to make anklets, toe-rings and earrings, and pawn them for paltry amounts—1,000 to 2,000 rupees. He gave us tea and told us that he was once a poet and a founding member of the Democratic Writers' Association of Jamshedpur. He then pulled out the Delhi edition of the *Rashtriya Sahara* which had printed my article.

My first report had been published not by the *Purvanchal Prahari* or some editor from Delhi but by a newspaper owned by a para-banking company, edited by a cartoonist. The article had then been picked up by the newspaper owned by the powerful businessman from Assam. After gossiping about authors who were mutual acquaintances, Bachcha Prasad proposed: He would not mortgage our ornaments, but he would loan us 1,000 rupees. Further, he would preserve cuttings of all our published articles. When we left the Northeast, we could 'buy back' our cuttings from him. He was a rare gold merchant, Bachcha Prasad, for whom our reports were precious jewellery.

From Bachcha Prasad's store I went straight to the office of the *Purvanchal Prahari* and confronted its owner G.L. Agarwala: Why was he printing my reports without permission? I hoped to put pressure on him for an advance and secure a commitment for future publication of my writing. Sweating rivers from the heat induced by the tamul he consumed, the massively built Agarwala calmly said he paid no one for their reports or their pieces and wouldn't pay me either. But, in return for writing for his newspaper, I could stay in his bureau offices in the Northeast and use his reporters as guides.

This was a precious windfall, much more valuable than cash, which I was receiving quite providentially. I immediately agreed and left, for the problem of the hotel bill remained unsolved. Shashwat emerged from his low blood pressure and phoned a journalist, who had also been his classmate, in Delhi. This journalist phoned Lata Umbrey, an MP from Arunachal Pradesh. The MP instructed one of his supporters in Guwahati, a travel agent, to give us 10,000 rupees. The man arrived in our hotel in three hours with the money. We never met MP Lata Umbrey, either before or after he arranged the money for us, but he was the invisible guardian angel who bailed us out of trouble. We never got the chance to even thank him.

~

We vacated the Janata Hotel. That night we boarded a bus. The plan now was to tour Upper Assam. In an upbeat mood, gazing at the lighthouses on the Brahmaputra shrouded in mist, hearing the whistles of the steamers, we reached the guesthouse built on the upper floor of the Jorhat office of the Purvanchal Prahari at 5 a.m. and set up quarters in the room favoured by G.L. Agarwala himself.

The almirahs in the room were full of incense sticks, candles, sprays of all kinds, many unintelligible court documents in English and Assamese, and clothes. We immediately began using the articles we needed. But all our efforts at sprucing up were in vain. That day the All Assam Students' Union (AASU) had called for a bandh to protest the murders of Hindi-speakers. Bandhs in the Northeast are utterly successful. On bandh days, not even a leaf stirs.

The office was downstairs and the guesthouse upstairs. All one needed to do was to sit downstairs, clad in G.L. Agarwala's broad-hemmed pyjamas, and the local news would come drifting in. One of the reporters, Kalita, said that an elderly correspondent from Delhi was stuck in a hotel because of the bandh. We thought, Let's go find out what a Delhi-walla is looking for in Jorhat.

In a coincidence, the man turned out to be a newly made friend of mine, Harishchandra Chandola who, at five in the afternoon, was peering into a laptop screen and trying to mix rice and an omelet on a plate. He had received this oddly matched dish only now because the bazaar had remained shut all day.

Speaking about Harishchandra Chandola six months earlier in Bareilly, Viren Dangwal—my former editor and a poet whom I dearly love—had said, 'Chandola, after a long reporting career covering many countries, especially the war-torn Gulf, is now growing potatoes in Joshimath. He has to stay up nights to protect his potato crop from marauding bears.' I had gone up to Joshimath to meet Chandola and found that he had left for Dehradun. That day, the first government of Uttarakhand was being sworn in. When I finally met him, I found that he had spent a significant portion of his life in the Northeast. In the sixties, he had been the Kohima correspondent for *The Times of India*. Prime Minister Lal Bahadur Shastri had appointed him mediator between Naga rebels and the government. He had married a Naga girl there.

Chandola was to go to Burma Camp (Dimapur) where he had to attend a marriage in a Naga relative's house. He gave us a week's notice: If we could reach Burma Camp, he promised to show us Khonoma, said to be the cradle of militancy in the Northeast. Khonoma is a historically significant village inhabited by the Angami tribe where, in October 1879, farmers had killed G.H. Damant, the first British Collector of Kohima. Khonoma was burnt down several times; first by the British, and then, after Independence, by the Indian Army.

~

After a cursory survey of the neglected houses of the old elites of Assam in the neighbourhoods before us, and of the black and brown backs of the children of Biharis swimming in the muck of the Bhogdoi River, we had no option but to make our way to Majuli.

Majuli is the world's largest river island and the religious nerve centre of Assam. Our guess was that the religious mutths on the island were the real museums which showcased Assamese culture. The museum in Guwahati and the state-endorsed literature there had thrown us into despair.

According to the flood control department of Assam, in 1950, the island used to be 1,250 square kilometres in size which, according to the Geological Survey of India, had reduced to 800 square kilometres. According to a rough estimate, in previous years, about 5 kilometres of land and 125 villages had been swallowed up by the river. I had a doubt in my mind that is used to the thrill of the rebellion of hope amidst negative fantasies: Assam can always be seen, but this natural miracle created by the Brahmaputra, Kherkutia and Subansiri Rivers may not remain forever?

That morning we expressed our gratitude to the two stubborn, average-sized bulls at the Neemati Ghat who had stalled the movement and helped us catch the steamer even though we were late. Tens of people were tugging at their ropes, cursing, and the bulls were backing up from the jetty with matched steps, full of fear. After about half an hour of tug-of-war, one made a panicked jump on to the steamer. The other preened, then walked up coolly on his own, as if to say, 'This is how one walks on water.'

Both doors to the cabin of the steamer were jammed shut with people. Outside, bulletins about the natures of bulls and goats were being broadcast in accordance with the rules written in the *Samudrik Shastra*. The narrow deck was crammed with bicycles, vegetables and bundles of household items on which people were sitting, gawking and laughing at an old drunk's 'theatre of parental affection'. He was seated in the middle, clutching a torn and dirty handmade doll. He cleaned its nose, bathed it, combed its hair, lovingly fed it rice, sent it off to school and then, all at once, began to slap it—the girl, like her mother before her, had emptied his bottle of homebrew into a drain. A schoolboy explained that two years earlier, the man's daughter had succumbed to snakebite. Since then he roamed all over, the ragdoll in hand.

Some time after noon, a dilapidated minibus traversed the burning sands of Majuli, swaying like an elephant, and dropped us near a footpath which would take us to the Natun Kamalabari Satra. Our bags and briefcases had rolled into all corners of the bus and it took us about twenty minutes to identify and claim them.

Before we could receive the key to a small room in the outside portion of the mutth, we had to submit to an interview with the satraadhikari, the head official of the Kamalabari Satra, Mahant Narayan Chandra Dev Goswami. He said: 'I know reporter people indulge. But as long as you stay here, you will not eat meat or drink alcohol.'

'So shall it be, Maharaj.' Saying this in a reassuring voice, I fingered the outline of the bottle of rum in my bag, which I had bought in Jorhat the previous day just in case thinking, Who knows, Majuli may not have a single store. Mahant Narayan Chandra Dev Goswami was built like an athlete, and fragments of unhusked paddy were entangled in his long hair. His laughter possessed a rare asceticism and in his manner of speaking was a simplicity which had remained intact even in this day and age. Quite naturally, I remembered those bejewelled, potbellied preachers, surrounded by rifles, always travelling in long cars who, were they to stand at this spot, would look like hoodlums black-marketing tickets to heaven.

Bundles of paddy were heaped in the mutth. One one side, paddy was being threshed. Sadhus, carrying sickles, and rope to tie paddy-bundles with, were walking to and fro. The Mahant, one of the more prominent poets of Assam, was, at that moment, engaged in the counting of paddy-bundles and the reckoning of diesel used for the pump. He gave us a long list of the articles of historical significance that the Archaeological Survey of India had asked them to safeguard, which were kept in the various mutths. He also showed us a photocopy of an Assamese newspaper, *Assam Vilasini*. This was the second newspaper published in the Assamese language which was brought out in 1871 from the Auniati Royal Satra in Majuli. The first newspaper, *Arunoday*, was published by the Baptist missionary Miles Bronson.

In the middle of the mutth was a massive, ancient

naamghar built upon wooden stilts. Mridang, cymbals, flutes, and many other unknown musical instruments had been placed everywhere on the floor which was plastered with cowdung. There were no idols or any paraphernalia used for rituals. This mutth was a collective of sadhus—followers of the tradition laid down by Sankar Dev, the great social reformer of the sixteenth century—who toiled and sweated like peasants for their livelihoods and practiced meditation in the Vaishnavite traditions. Krishna is their personal deity, and their devotion is expressed in immersive kirtan-singing. Sankar Dev had propagated this new religion through dramas, songs and poems. He had also evolved a new dance-form, the 'satriya' which, after receiving governmental recognition, was being taught in dance schools nowadays.

Most Hindu Assamese villages are connected to some mutth or the other and the naamghar has a central role to play in the community life of the village. A naamghar is a verandah-like structure built on cement, wooden or bamboo stilts, open on three sides, where people gather to collectively perform kirtans. In gatherings which last from evening till late at night, people discuss domestic quarrels, local politics, militancy and other matters of the world. Nowadays, under the influence of Hindu fundamentalism, women are prevented from coming to the naamghar for five days of the month and this is being protested by city-based feminist organizations.

Behind the mutth, young, dhoti-clad, topless sadhus with tufts of hair on their tonsured heads were playing cricket on land from which paddy had been cleared. An immense bat, like the machete wielded by the demon

Mahishasur, had been made by hand. Bamboo wickets. From the leg-pads artfully woven out of straw, it could be deduced that LBW was a valid dismissal. With the cork ball landing on a dug-up field with the stumps of harvested rice plants, it was impossible to tell which delivery would end up a bouncer and which one a Yorker. This uncertainty had lent the game a spiritual air. Shashwat asked Kamalakant Saikia, who had recently been caught out and who sat on the boundary, crosslegged and glum, 'Sadhu-ji, when you have made such extensive arrangements, why not build yourself a proper pitch?'

'Guest, the number of runs a man will make in this life, and how he will get out, everything is preordained,' came his reply, made with supreme detachment.

One receding evening, I was sitting in that empty, lonely naamghar when a window, shut for ages, opened up in the darkness within me. A ray of light shafted in through a gap in the straw roof above—a blue straight footpath from space. Patches of sunlight crept secretly along on the cool, cowdung-plastered floor of the naamghar. If I would look at them, they would stop.

I found myself thinking, If I ever have a religion, it will be as simple, focused and pure. Pure! What is that? …But why don't you have a religion? Because religion brings along refined ways of hypocrisy, untouchability, fundamentalism, hatred, superstition and oppression. But these are not the faults of faith, these are crimes perpetrated by the shrewd *preachers* of faith. You can have an utterly personal faith which needs ratification from no one, can you not? Think, if such a thing were possible, you wouldn't be so pessimistic, lonely and without alternatives. Your life might have a purpose. This was a terrifying thought which had assumed gale force and was touching the arid cracks of my innermost being. I shivered. I was afraid. Had the seed of spirituality taken root within me. I looked around… Where is the harm in living an aimless life? I pulled out a hip-flask from my trouser pocket, quickly swigged a mouthful of rum, and stepped out.

~

What is being done to stop the erosion of the Majuli Island, which supports a population of one-and-a-half lakh people? And why are entire Mishing villages converting to Christianity? These two curiosities led us to two Mahantas. One was Manik Mahanta, executive engineer of the flood control department, who told us that the Brahmaputra Board had been set up in 1975 to study the problem.

'A study that has lasted twenty-five years?'

'But look at the size of the problem!'

The other was a local leader, Professor Pratul Mahanta—a man of simple heart—who did not volunteer any information but made two bicycles available to us, implying, go see for yourselves. When Shashwat said he didn't know how to ride a bicycle at all, the professor agreed to come along. He first showed me a mated pair of shelducks on the riverside, which was a very significant sighting for me. For thirty years I had been reading about these birds in poems and love songs—immortalized as the ill-fated 'chakwa-chakai' bird-pair—which I saw for the first time in Majuli. The chakwa-chakai is a species of duck.

In the middle of the island, built upon fertile land and

surrounded by trees, was a group of 150-year-old mutths set up by Sankar Dev. Mishing villages stood upon the sandy shores of the river; crosses made out of tinselly plastic gleamed on the huts there. Between the mutths and the villages were little ponds, paddy fields and small woods where a rich wealth of migratory birds had descended. The river stretched all around their gentle murmurs. Before us was an endless blue gleam. The bicycle would hum along over greenery but, on the sand of the river bank, it would dig its wheels in like a stubborn animal and refuse to move.

In the Dakhinpat and Bengniati satras were displayed ancient manuscripts written on leaves of the sanchi plant. They also stored the armours, crowns, mirrors, votive lights, paan-containers etcetera—all of which smelled of napthalene—that belonged to the Ahom kings and their prominent courtiers. These articles seemed devalued because of the running commentary of the sadhus. For them, these were objects which were to be bartered for something more valuable in future. The neglect on the part of the government was the priests' chief obsession and their immediate centre of hope was the UNO, where the application to have Majuli declared a World Heritage Site had been languishing for years. Sensing our boredom, Pratul Mahanta took us to a government official's house for a cup of tea.

It was a small bungalow, shaded by coconut and areca-nut trees, and the fragrance of local roses ran riot in the small lawn outside. Chrysanthemum, dahlia and bougainvillea were in blossom, and some quacking ducks, each blaming the other for her plumpness, busily waddled about. Then the fragrance of mutton being cooked slipped out through half-open windows, ruffling the white curtains on its way, reached the verandah and wafted Shashwat to his grandmother's lap and the laps of all the women ancestors of his family. Of necessity, all of those women were shy, culinary experts, hospitable, and ah! the meat and the fish curry cooked by their hands, how delicious they were! Modern women, he felt, don't know what they have lost by neglecting the kitchen. Even if they earn a lot of money and put a dog-leash on their men's collars and take them every morning for a walk, they will never be able to understand the joy felt by those ancient Annapurnas, those hoary goddesses of plenty. Anyway, within half an hour we were seated at the dining table. Exclaiming, 'Bhal hoise, khoob bhal hoise' (This is good... truly excellent), we polished off quantities of mutton and rice. Afterwards, Shashwat stretched out on the verandah and snored. It was a sweet day, a 'malai sumsum' day.

In the Mishing village were herds upon herds of naked and half-naked children whose only attire that might be deemed social were their bright smiles. Inside the huts, the adults were weaving the finest, most valuable fabric in the world. Sitting underneath a hut was a sickly woman with a torn mekhla (a sarong) tied over her breasts, spinning muga silk on a loom. A Jesus Christ calendar fluttered opposite her. Her husband and children were sitting outside, searching for lice in each other's hair. Not only had their religion changed, polyester threads were accompanying the silk. Cheap dye was being used in place of natural colours. Handloom is—after tea, gas and oil—the most lucrative industry in Assam sustaining the livelihoods of lakhs of tribals. I gestured at the Jesus Christ calendar many times before the woman understood my drift. She said with a forced smile: 'We are not Hindu.'

'Why did you become Christian?'

'What to do? No choice.' She pointed to her children.

'Go to the satra. To the Dakhinpat naamghar.'

'That... that is for high-caste Hindus. They will chase us away from there.'

Wading in knee-deep water in the wetland outside the village, bird-lover Tilak Sarmah of the Assam Science Society identified numerous migratory birds for us. These birds hadn't come there like we had—to wander about in our dark futures—but to hatch their children and to have them fly alongside on their way back. The most remarkable of the birds among the many which were there were the great adjutant storks who have a massive pouch hanging from their necks. In the Army, an adjutant is an officer's assistant. Carrion-eaters, these massive birds sometimes accompany vultures. Because their legs don't bend, there is a military quality about their gait. Human beings have still not been able to understand the use of their pouches. But this bird is useful in many black magic totems.

Just to tease him, I asked an elderly tribal man catching fish in a pool. 'What should be done to arrest the erosion of Majuli Island?'

He answered with a counter-question, 'Why are you so worried about Majuli?'

'Meaning?'

'If man didn't create this island, why does he try to save it?'

'Then?'

'The rivers who created this island will wipe it away. They will make a new one and we will go live there.'

~

As the landscape changes, so do our half-formed impressions and notions.

The earthen hillocks of middling height take our polite leave, and the plateau of Karbi Anglong starts. The greenery of the North Cachar Hills glimmers in the background. The Assam we left behind in the plains, the Assam which complains of Delhi's domination, emerges here as a regional strongman. For decades, slogans have been etched on walls in this area demanding a separate state in protest against the imposition of the Assamese language and the 'Assamization' of tribal culture.

Karbi Anglong and North Cachar Hills are administered by autonomous councils which control all aspects of governance except law and order, supplies, excise, polls and census. These councils fix their own budgets but have to have them passed by the Assam Legislative Assembly. In the Barak Valley, no one addresses these two areas as districts; they have given themselves the status of 'sub-states' which continue to struggle to attain full statehood. Before the British arrived in 1850, there were Karbi kings whose capital was Diphu. The king of North Cachar was from the Dimasa tribe and Dimapur used to be their capital.

'Jayanta Rongpi murdabad!' This was one slogan among the many written on the walls. In places 'murdabad' had been deleted and replaced with 'zindabad'. Rongpi is the MP from Karbi and a leader of the Autonomous State Demand

Committee whom I had once met in Delhi. According to Rongpi, the Assamese people from the plains consider the hill tribals—who are of Indo-Mongol origin—uncivilized which is why, in Karbi, up to 90 per cent of all the official posts in the government have been filled up by the Assamese and most of the government contracts are awarded to them. Rongpi is a Naxal Communist; according to the members of his party, the Assam government nominates its stooges in the councils on the condition that they tarnish the image of the tribal leaders.

The North Cachar Hills is populated by the Dimasa, the Zeme Naga, the Hmar, the Kuki and Karbi tribes. In this area, which abuts the Sylhet district of Bangladesh, the issues of language and culture become even more complicated. The Cachari tribals speak Dimasa which is written in the Bangla script. The medium of instruction in schools is Bangla, Assamese and English, but the local radio station broadcasts its programmes in a patois called 'Haflong Hindi'. Because of the open border with Bangladesh, the Cachar area is a transit zone for Naga, Meitei and Kuki militants. The kidnapping of opponents, the extortion of 'loyalty tax' from businesspeople, and the murder of informers is common and not paid much attention to.

Tribal communities which have smaller populations have banded together to form new alliances and are demanding recognition of their languages and autonomous territories of their own. Their strategy is an ancient one—they believe that just as a mother will not breastfeed her child until it cries, so will the Centre not pay them attention until they rattle arms. Three Naga tribes, the Zeme, the Liangmei and the Rongmei have come together to become the 'Zeliangrong'. The Chokri, the Khezha and the Sangtam have banded together to form the 'Chakhesang'. Three villages in Nagaland—Sapo, Kechuri and Khuri—are collectively called 'Pochuri'. There cannot be even an iota of doubt that the Northeast is Asia in miniature. There is almost no Asian community whose forefathers were not here, whose words and languages don't find reflection and inclusion in the languages spoken here, and in whose religious beliefs one will not see a clear non-Aryan, non-Dravidian stamp. There are even a few tribal communities who are in touch with Israel. They seek their origins among the Jews.

Wherever the bus would stop, I would run to a PCO to call Harishchandra Chandola and tell him that we were on our way to Dimapur. But there would be long queues in front of each that included people from gaonburas (headmen) or children with schoolbags slung on their backs.

Star Plus had set up special phone lines for Assam. Everyone, be they from the plains, the Cachar, or the hills, wanted to try their luck with *Kaun Banega Crorepati? (KBC)*, the quiz programme. The chief topic of discussion in these queues was the general knowledge (GK) of those people who, because they couldn't answer the easy questions put to them by *KBC* host Amitabh Bachchan, would lose the lakhs of rupees already in their pockets and come away empty-handed. Seated in teashops a little distance away from the queues, film experts of the village were dispensing special wisdom to teenagers on Amitabh Bachchan's voice, the wig on 'Laambu's' head which cost many crores, and

Rekha's 'bhootjolokiya' love, as hot as the legendary Ghost Chili.

At a halt just before Diphu, a tribal man came trundling up on his bicycle, looking for his son who was testing his GK against other boys standing in a queue. Long bamboo canes were clamped under the bicycle's carrier and a bunch of long-stemmed light-yellow flowers dangled from the canes. The boy had just caught hold of another to take his place, and was looking to slip away, when his father caught sight of him and ran with a cane upraised. The boy fled but the father sank down to the ground, holding his head in his hands, before he reached his son. He was terrified of the bamboo flowers. He had told his son to chop down their bamboo and set fire to the stumps; however, the boy had come to the PCO to dial that number which had the magical ability to make him a crorepati. This had been going on for many days.

He threw the cane to the ground and lamented, 'Not even god will put a morsel of food into the mouths of the children of the man who ignores the fire raging in his own house and runs off to gamble with a horse-faced stranger!'

The people who were gathered, and even the man's son, laughed the description of Amitabh Bachchan, but they also knew that the pretty bamboo flowers were harbingers of destruction. At that time bamboo plants were flowering in some parts of North Cachar Hills and Karbi Anglong. The agricultural department of the Assam government had instructed all its offices that they should do everything within their power to destroy the groves of flowering bamboo.

Of all the flora growing upon the soil of the Northeast,

the most visible are bamboo and areca-nut. The bamboo is as integral to life in the region as those arteries which carry blood all over the body. Bamboo finds many uses—in Meghalaya as irrigation channels; as pipelines which bring rainwater to remote villages in Mizoram; as knives in Nagaland; and as utensils in some areas. The power of destruction contained within its flowers is terrifying. It is a mystery—like a trilling flute which, on striking a certain note, transforms into a neck-severing sword.

These flowers come rarely but when they do, they create a new imbalance in nature. Rats eat the bamboo flowers which unnaturally amps up their reproductive power. These rodents in their lakhs go through anything that comes their way—standing crops, stored-up grain, fruits, vegetables—in an all-consuming hunger. Famine strikes within a year of flowering. The elders of the tribal communities told us that most of the bamboo groves in the region would flower over the following three years. If all the groves weren't burnt down, destruction was assured.

These were the flowers which had set the foundations of militancy in Mizoram and which changed both the history and the geography of the Northeast. Mizoram was then one of the districts of Assam and used to be known as the Lushai Hills.

In 1959, rats fresh off a bamboo-flower feast attacked fields, forests and human settlements; famine loomed. The Mizos fled towards villages in the Cachar areas but the local populace and the Assam Police pushed them back. Mizo leaders pleaded with the Assam government for help. By the time the administrative machinery could grind into action, the sturdy foundations of bloodshed which would last for the next twenty-five years had been cast. Citizens, despairing of the government, formed crisis organizations. One among these groups was the Mizo Famine Front (MFF) which had been put together by Laldenga, an ex-clerk of Havildar rank in the Army. Cobbling together a network of former soldiers and young volunteers, Laldenga arranged to send grain to far-flung villages. These veterans would occasionally carry a message along with the rations: 'The governments of Assam and India do not care about starving, dying Mizos. The time has come for us to fight for a separate country.' Eventually, the MFF became the Mizo National Front (MNF) and began to demand secession from India to form a separate country for the Mizos. To the Indian government, this demand was a clerk's whim, and was brushed aside.

Laldenga and his boys contacted the ISI and reached Chittagong in East Pakistan. Having learned the use of arms and guerilla warfare there, they began to attack police outposts in Mizoram. In February 1966 they conducted Operation Jericho and, one night, managed to stun the entire nation by capturing the radio station, the treasury and the police station in Aizawl. Laldenga gave this attack a religious colour to get support from the Christian population. In scripture, Prophet Joshua, under orders from the Supreme Father, brought down the walls of the fort of Jericho so that the devotees of the Supreme Father could have their own homeland.

Helicopters of the Indian Air Force were used for the first time in India against a militant organization to take back control of Aizawl. For the next five years, the Army set up one Protected Progressive Village (PPV) after the other while the MNF kept up a steady guerilla war. Here, PPVs are compared to Hitler's Nazi camps. All the villages of Mizoram were uprooted and the people were relocated to tin sheds by roadsides which had been set up so that contact between militants and the common people could be prevented. Movement without showing identity cards was impossible. Under the Army's persistently sadistic surveillance, people forgot the meaning of privacy. The oppression further alienated citizens from the Centre. The MMF, in the meantime, had set up seven battalions in the jungles of Burma and Laldenga was in China talking to Chou En Lai. The Mizo claim that they originated from a cave called Chinlung in China. In a journey that would have lasted centuries, they are said to have crossed the Tibetan plateau, and the Kabaw and Hukawng valleys of Burma to reach and settle in the Lushai Hills in the eighteenth century.

These villages were resettled in a few years. In 1985 Mizoram had to be hived off into a separate state. In 1987, after Prime Minister Rajiv Gandhi and Laldenga struck a deal, the chief minister, who was from the Congress Party, had to be removed and Laldenga installed as CM in his place. By then, the Army had destroyed communal life within the villages. Crime exploded and half of Mizoram uprooted itself to settle in three cities. Almost every citizen domiciled in Mizoram—including militants—was compensated for some damage or the other because of which corruption has become a synonym for Mizoram. Aizawl is now counted as the most expensive Indian city to live in where the population of drug addicts is very high.

~

At first glance, from the thick layer of dust on houses, the trucks upon the potholed roads, and the dishevelled people with tangled hair, the first town in Nagaland, Dimapur, appears like a godown of a transport company. Dimapur is also an old centre of trade, situated outside the Inner Line, and the final railway station on that route in the Northeast. The English had etched the Inner Line in 1873 to prevent the Nagas from attacking the border areas of Assam and Manipur. The raiding Nagas would loot not just goods and wealth but carry away heads too. Even today, every Indian, before entering Nagaland, is required to secure an Inner Line Permit declaring the reason for the journey and the duration of the stay—Harishchandra Chandola had secured ours before we arrived. 'A permit? To travel in one's own country?'—on asking this question, someone or the other replies with the simplicity of a child building sandcastles: 'You have left your country behind. From here on is the home of the Nagas.' Some hopeful face or the other warns every newcomer: 'Don't be out on the streets after the lights have been turned on for the night. Anything may happen.'

The fear that anything may happen is exaggerated. What actually happens is that after dusk, small bands of local drug addicts might waylay a lone traveller and loot his money. Or snatch his mobile phone or watch. If the man protests, they might even beat him a little. Also, at every checkpost, Army jawans strictly detain, search and interrogate all travellers. The religious-minded who must pass through the neighbourhood of Sema Nagas which falls between the railway station and Burma Camp read the *Hanuman Chalisa* even in daytime. The boys of the Sema tribe are infamous.

We had a telephone number to call for the address of one of Harishchandra Chandola's Naga relatives in Burma Camp—we were to make our way there. As I dialled, I glimpsed ruptured national integration twinkling in a pair of slitted, innocent eyes, a twinkle which was yet only a raw impulse. Once the teenaged girl manning the PCO found that we had come from Delhi, she asked shyly, 'Can you give me Rittik Roshan's most personal phone number?'

'I could, but his daddy has forbidden us to share his number with girls from the Northeast.'

'Why?'

'Because you eat tamul, that's why.'

'Not me.' She bared her milky white teeth.

'My mobile phone network is not working. Dial my number …'

'Your beard is already white. I don't want your number, just his.' She laughed heartily for a while after saying that. I then remembered that Hrithik Roshan's debut film *Kaho Na Pyar Hai* and its title song had both become superhits.

Shashwat said that we should go to Harishchandra Chandola's relative looking like gentlemen so our bags were tossed down to the ground in front of a hair-cutting saloon. The barber was a man from a village near Patna, a devout vegetarian Hindu who occasionally ate eggs. With shampoo in our hair and beards, he settled us in a meditative posture and began his epic narration to illustrate how difficult life in Dimapur is, one which still comes to me in my dreams. I was spellbound by the troughs and crests of his voice, which lightly wheezed and shivered from asthma and kept pace with the delicate snip-snip of his scissors.

'About ten days ago, an Assamese man arrived in Dimapur on an elephant, laden with rice... He was on his way back to Assam after selling the rice when one of the elephant's hind legs got caught in a joint in the tracks near the outer signal of the station. He sat for a long time in front of the station-master's office, pleading with the babus that they free his elephant. No one heard the poor man. After persistent pleading, the station-master said, "You will have to go to Guwahati to get the Big Officer's order." An incoming train had to be shunted for the foot to be extracted from the tracks. The mahout cut down pipal branches for the elephant, caressed its forehead, and rushed off to Guwahati in a hired jeep. There the mahout left and here people from the Sema village fell upon the elephant with machetes and knives. Thousands gathered to gawk when they heard the trumpeting. Even as they looked, the Sema hacked the elephant into little pieces. After three hours, thirty-five minutes and seventeen seconds, there was no trace of the elephant. The Semas divided all the meat amongst themselves and carried it home in huge baskets. The mahout came back in the evening to find one ear of his elephant lying on the platform like a forgotten handkerchief and went mad with shock.'

This story was the first thing I told Christian Aunty and wanted to know if it was true.

'Semas can eat anything. And elephant meat isn't half bad,' she said.

We were guests of Christian Aunty, a woman who wore chintz frocks, spoke convent-school English, and had an open mind whose children lived and worked abroad. Decorated with a cross, a Bible, a guitar, illustrated

Easter eggs and photographs taken in front of assorted churches, hers was a typical Christian household in which, at breakfast and at dinner, all the forgotten good manners had to be first remembered and then diligently practised. Over twelve hours Christian Aunty told us that there are thirty-two Naga tribes of whom five live in Burma, sixteen in Nagaland, seven in Manipur, three in the Tirap region of Arunachal Pradesh and one in the Karbi and North Cachar areas of Assam. Of these, she reported 'ninety-eight per cent' to be Christian. In a heartfelt manner, she repeated in English, twice: 'From very ancient times they are self-esteemed and freedom-spirited people.'

That evening we accompanied Harishchandra Chandola to the hotel where he was staying with a friend. It was seven, and dusty, crowded Dimapur had undergone radical transformation. It was as if curfew had been clamped upon the town and darkness had given the place a mysterious air. Thrice jawans of the Army halted our car at barriers and peered inside. They were hunting two Sema boys who, only a few hours earlier, had looted a stranger and vanished. The only flourishing location in seedy Dimapur was the Bata Chowk where a few girls with rough hair were standing outside a shuttered liquor store. Their going rate was 200 rupees and a nip—a 90 ml measure of liquor. Popping little chewing-gum balloons, the girls were inviting Army jawans with small, languid movements of their heads. These were alcohol- and drug-addicted girls from poverty-stricken families, and, from their cruel eyes, it was hard to tell if it was their bodies they were selling or something else.

~

On the 78-kilometre highway to Kohima, lined by the towering walls of the farmhouses of Naga ministers and officers, we came across only three civilian cars and one elephant which were journeying in the opposite direction. We could see the head of a one-tusked elephant behind tall bushes on a hill slope. Either the elephant was patiently waiting for our taxi to pass, and then to cross the road, or it was plunged deep into the dilemmas which must have faced the first Naga to have settled in Nagaland.

According to myth, the first Naga was called either Koja or Khoja and he had come there from the east. There is a place in Manipur called Mekroma; when he reached this place, Koja could not decide how to proceed. He finally prayed to god for guidance. A bird settled on the horn of his mithun (an animal from the cow family) then flew off in the direction of where Khezhakhonoma is today. To be doubly sure, Koja tossed his staff into the air. It also landed pointing in the direction which the bird had taken. Taking it to be a sign from the spirit world, he walked in that direction. At one place, Koja came across a frog which brought him a grain of rice. Koja took the grain of rice and placed it upon a rock after which it split into two. Koja settled there with his wife. They had numerous children. When the children quarreled over who would offer the first grains of rice from the first harvest to the sacred stone, Koja's wife lit a fire underneath it. The stone shattered into several pieces. Recognizing this as a sign from the ancestors, Koja's children struck out in different directions and settled down to become the Naga tribes we know today. In Khezhakhonoma is a large rock which the

Nagas worship. It is said that the Ao tribe was the first to arrive, followed by the Lotha, the Sema, the Rengma, the Angami and the Chakhesang tribes. The Ao, who are the most educated and serve in government jobs, claim their origins from the megaliths of Langtorek.

These same-looking hills, all rolling one after the other; which one was best to settle down on? One knows of this dilemma from stories, as well as the fragmentation of a people into various tribes in search of land and livelihood but one question remains unanswered: How did the tribes end up speaking such different languages? The Naga tribes don't just not understand each other's words, they don't understand each other's feelings too; there are many long-running small-scale wars between them. Even Naga historians rue the lack of a pan-Naga language as the biggest obstacle to nation-building. Knotty tribal histories cannot be understood through academic perspectives or with academic tools. That which we seek on paper is written in the wind, the water and the leaves and constantly changes. No tongue in Nagaland includes the word 'Naga'. This is a word given to them by outsiders and no one knows what it actually means.

As dusk gathered, Harishchandra Chandola said, 'If we had arrived a little later, Kohima would have looked like the Milky Way from where we stand.' His voice held something of the excitement of a man coming home. Every church tower we passed on our way was brightly illuminated and bore aloft one shimmering star each. Christmas was due in two days. We were headed to Khonoma.

~

The following morning began with the infuriating feeling of having been duped which took me to the petty criminal trade practices that necessarily continue under the cover of militancy.

I had hoped to see a bit of Kohima before travelling on to Khonoma. But, that morning, the toothpaste tasted of chalk and stuck to my gums like glue. The bathing soap did not lather at all—nearly as hard as stone, it bruised my skin. The cold cream wouldn't ooze out at all—the tube remained stone-like even when I hit it with my fist. It was a while before the hotel would serve breakfast and I wanted to nibble on a biscuit but it was of the same chalky family as the toothpaste.

All these articles had been bought the previous day from a general store in front of the hotel. The thug Marwari shopkeeper could be seen through a small window in the store, waving incense in front of the statues of Lakshmi and Ganesh. I decided to make a consumer rights intervention before he could make his first auspicious sale of the day.

Tossing the useless goods on to his counter, I said, 'You loot.'

No expression crossed the Marwari's face. One by one, he waved incense in front of each of the fake goods he held in stock and prayed to both the gods for all of them to sell at their full prices. After offering the incense sticks at the feet of the gods he went to the back of his store and emerged with a tube of toothpaste in hand. 'This is my personal toothpaste, you can have it. I cannot do any more for you. The underground and over-ground outfits here charge us so much tax that business has become impossible. Bhaisahab, if I sell original articles, I'll starve.

You will find this happening all over Kohima, in every store. At times we get a few original articles but I don't have them in stock right now.' He bared his teeth at me. He was pleased that this final round of polite duplicity had gone off well.

The Sardar from the shop next door interrupted his wiping down the bottles of soda, cold drinks and Bisleri and came over in support of the Marwari shopkeeper. 'Sahib, we're only businessmen; here, even the cops pay taxes. Everything is taxed; televisions, fridges, scooters, cars... They accept anything as tax: chickens, goats, pigs, grain. Here you either go "herbal" or you start eating and drinking like the Nagas do. Only then is survival possible.'

'What is "herbal"?'

'A few steps from here is a football field. Behind the field is a vegetable market, and there you find "herbal" in plenty.'

Ninety per cent of the economy of Nagaland runs on the grants given to the state by the Centre. Any delay in the grant precipitates a financial crisis. In 1994, a fortnight's delay meant that the government ran out of money to pay salaries and the employees of the secretariat went on strike. Then, the chief minister had been found saying 'on record' in a meeting of the heads of various government departments, 'I have confirmed information that you people are slipping a portion of the state budget to militants and causing the state harm.'

It is an open secret that Grade-IV officials give 10 per cent of their salary as tax; Grade-II officials 20 per cent; and Grade-I officials a minimum of 30 per cent. Alongside runs the parallel extortion racket run by those hoodlums pretending to represent the underground. The leaders and officials are not worried at all that money belonging to the government is being siphoned off to militants. Corruption has crossed all limits. And even the most corrupt official repeats like a parrot: 'India keeps Nagaland not because the state contributes to the national economy but for political reasons. This money is sent by Delhi to keep Naga citizens tame. If someone wants to pocket a bit of it, we have no problem with that.'

Tax-collection often brings destruction in its wake. Every militant organization wants to maintain its hold on Moreh because Moreh is one of the largest centres for the cross-border smuggling of drugs and other contraband. When the NSCN (Nationalist Socialist Council of Nagaland) clashes with Kuki militants over tax-collection in Moreh, Naga-Kuki clashes break out in Manipur, Nagaland and North Cachar. Women and children are butchered, villages are torched, and ideologues on both sides start spinning political and sociological theories about the massacres.

I had subconsciously resolved to find a local 'datun', a twig to clean my teeth with, or to not brush as long as I was in Nagaland; perhaps this was why I followed the Sardar's directions. Colourful birds from dozens of species were strung up on wire garlands for sale in the vegetable market. Naga women would shake the garlands in front of prospective customers; the birds' heads would loll about and their beaks would fall open. Who knew, perhaps these garlands also included the famous hornbill, whose vibrantly colourful feathers Nagas use in their headdresses. The Hornbill Festival, held at the end of the year, is named after this bird. Around this time, pictures of spear-wielding

Naga dancers in colourful costumes make their way all over the world. It was that time of the year when frogs lie in hibernation but even they had been brought to the market for sale. The live earthworms, snails, tortoises and wasp hives were crawling about in their baskets between the inert potatoes, cauliflowers, turnips and tomatoes as if to furnish evidence of their being alive. Dried fish, brought here from elsewhere, stared wide-eyed at the culinary culture of this new place where, on Valentine's Day, restaurants welcome lovers with a signboard that says 'Dog Meat Special'. 'Sooka Roti People' is a name given to that special species of human which remains totally vegetarian.

There are woodlands here and human settlements. In between them is the howl of the wind and the rain. That which gives meaning to life—birdsong and the comings and goings of animals—is missing. This is because the Nagas are born hunters. On their part, the Nagas protest that this is not so, not all birds and animals have been hunted down. Deer, tigers, elephants, mithuns and many different bird species abound in dense forests but there they are on higher ground, and away from the hunters' shadow. The hunters' reach extends to these forests too, and prey is brought back from there. A mithun skull is a favoured door ornament of the Nagas. And while head-hunting was banned during the British Raj, human skulls are carefully preserved in homes as precious heirlooms. The heads of enemies heads used to be offered to the earth-god with prayers for fertility of every kind. So many spears, machetes, bows, knives and guns can be seen in an average Naga household, it seems like a weapon museum. A major part of these collections are made up of those arms and ammunition which were left behind after the Second World War. Households which don't possess real guns keep wooden replicas.

From the 'herbal' in the vegetable market I understood why the road from Dimapur to Kohima had been silent. Birds and animals knew from generations of experience: However poetic the contents of the glossy documents borne aloft by well-meaning wildlife lovers and environmentalists, once they crossed the Inner-Line barrier in Chumuekdima, they could never go back alive.

~

On travelling to Khonoma, whether by road, or by the slim pathways which wind up alongside terraced fields, or over the cobblestones of memory, an encounter with history is inevitable. Near the principal fortress in town is a stone on which the following text is inscribed: 'G.H. Damant, MACS, Killed at Khonoma, 4 October 1879'. 'Major C.R. Cock, Major H.H. Forbes (44th Garrison), Lieutenant Ridgeway (43 Bengal Infantry, Victoria Cross), Subedar Major Nurwar Sain (44th Garrison Gurkha Rifles) 22 November 1879'. A small finch hopped on to the stone; at the next bend in the road we came across two runny-nosed children who were stalking the finch, catapults in hand. Khonoma is surrounded by three forts, Mehrma, Semoma and Thoboma, which have been built upon three hills from which enemies marching upon the village could spotted from afar. Records of attacks mounted from Khonoma and defenses organized here are available for the last one-and-a-half centuries.

The English captured Assam in 1826; they encountered

the Nagas in 1832 when two officers of the British Army, Captains Jenkins and Pemberton, set out with 1,500 gunners and 800 coolies to find a route from Manipur to Assam. This military expedition, which left Imphal in January 1832, reached Assam in twenty-three days, travelling via Sengmae, Myang Khang, Merse, Khonoma, Nirema and Chumukedima. The Naga battled them with spears and arrows all the way. They hadn't yet ever seen rifles. The British shot and killed many people in Khonoma, which then comprised close to 400 houses. Military campaigns were an almost annual affair in Khonoma from then up to 1950 and the British burnt the village down twice. However, the viceroy, Lord Dalhousie, had taken into consideration the enormous costs the British were paying in terms of financial resources and human lives and had declared that the tribes were to be left alone to war among themselves and that the government shouldn't interfere in inter-tribal conflicts. Trade would continue until peace lasted but, at the least unrest, British relations with the tribes would be severed. Colonel Johnston, an officer posted in Manipur, set this order aside to establish an administrative headquarters in Kohima.

On 10 December 1850, the British Army shelled the Khonoma fort all day with a mortar from a distance of 450 feet but couldn't breach the wall. Thirty-four soldiers died in the ten-hour-long battle. When the army entered the fort the following day, there was no one in it. All the residents of Khonoma had escaped into the forests in the upper reaches. After the destruction of Khonoma in 1850, the Nagas attacked the British-held areas of Assam and Manipur twenty-two times within a span of one year, killing fifty-five and taking 113 prisoner. Between 1854 and 1865, they killed or abducted 232 people in raids on British-held areas. In 1872, Major Godwin Austen (who measured the height of Mount Everest) was sent to survey the Naga Hills. The army forced Naga coolies at gunpoint to transport rations and equipment for the survey team but the Nagas could never understand how an outsider could survey their land. In 1875, the deputy commissioner Captain Butler reached Pangti—a village inhabited by Nagas of the Lotha tribe—with a survey team where their throats were cut. Pangti was torched too.

The first collector of Kohima, G.H. Damant, left for Khonoma on 3 October 1879 with eighty-one soldiers and coolies to demonstrate political dominance. He had received news that new guns had been bought in Khonoma. He halted for the night in Jotsoma village. When he was about to leave the following morning, a Naga translator held his hand and implored him not to go because the village was prepared for war. When Damant reached, he found the wooden gates of the village shut. As soon as he stood before the door, a shot rang out from behind it, hit Damant on the head, and he died on the spot. Attacking from their ambush positions behind megaliths—huge stones partially buried in the ground to commemorate community feasts—Nagas killed thirty-six of Damant's troops, including his three bodyguards, and injured twenty-nine others. The Nagas reached Kohima on 23 October and attacked the British fort there. One hundred soldiers remained trapped inside the fort until 2,000 troops from Manipur under the command of Colonel Johnston broke the siege and rescued them.

The British concluded that as long as Khonoma remained standing, they could find no foothold in the region. Consequently, preparations were made for one year. An army was put together under General Nation which included the 44th Sylhet Light Infantry under Colonel Natal, the 43 Assam Light Infantry under Major Evans, and two elephant-drawn cannons of the Royal Artillery commanded by Lieutenant Mansell. The British Army pounded the lower portions of the village with cannon fire and captured it. The residents fled to the upper reaches to escape the cannons. The entire village was burnt down, just as it had been in 1850. And, this time, the terraced fields and irrigation channels were also obliterated. To prevent aid from arriving, thirteen neighbouring villages including Pefema, Merema, Sachima, Sefema, Puchema and Jotsoma had already been razed. In retaliation, the residents of Khonoma kept tossing down rocks on the British from a height. In 1880, after the British Army had left, fifty warriors from Khonoma, armed with seven rifles, trekked 80 miles over four days through the jungles of Manipur to attack the Baladhan Tea Estate in Cachar. They burnt down the estate, killed the manager Mr Blythe along with sixteen labourers and carried away their heads.

The residents of Khonoma wandered about in the forests for one year after the attack. Many died of starvation, disease and injury. In February 1881, the Chief Commissioner of Assam, Sir Steuart Bayley, allowed residents to return to Khonoma on the following conditions: no houses could be built in the upper reaches; each family had to pay an annual tax of 40 kilogrammes of paddy, one silver rupee and provide a few days of labour per year. A chief was appointed to ensure compliance. Steuart Bayley's replacement as chief commissioner of Assam, Elliot surveyed Khonoma in March and was astonished to find people building straw houses and preparing to sow rice. In 1884, the British officer and historian Mackenzie wrote: 'There is hardly any other place where the administration has been as brutal as it has been in Khonoma! No means of livelihood has been left intact.'

A giant war memorial stands in Khonoma with the following words inscribed upon it: 'Those who died a hundred years ago so that we remain free, we haven't forgotten them. We remember them still, and we sing their songs.'

The next big attack mounted on Khonoma was by the Indian Army in 1956 in retaliation against the armed insurrection launched by Angami Zapu Phizo. The village burned yet again, its neighbours were razed once more, and the Angamis wandered about in the forests in the higher reaches. A memorial stands testimony to this battle as well; built in 1995, it carries the names of the forty-six who died fighting the Indian Army between 1956 and 1992. Visolino Doli is the lone woman among these names. People standing near the memorial said that it was only after the coming of the Indian Army that they came to know what rape was. Stonemason Bolai Meru was also in that group, whose brother Mehosile Meru was twelfth on that list of the dead. He walked back a few steps in respect and observed: 'All men seem the same once their names are carved into stone.'

In the forties, Phizo travelled to Burma to join the Japanese, who were then preparing to attack the British, in the hope that the Japanese would oust the British from the Naga territories. Phizo was arrested in 1945 and accused of being a spy for the Japanese. He returned home one year later to set up the Naga National Council (NNC), which declared Nagaland independent on 14 August 1947. On 16 May 1953, the NNC conducted a plebiscite in which it claimed that 99 per cent of the people of Nagaland had voted for a separate Naga country. The Nagas boycotted the first general elections of India. In 1954, Phizo announced the formation of the Government of Free Nagaland under the leadership of a fictional president, Hongkhin. By then, the Nagas had rounded up weapons left over after the Second World War and had begun skirmishes. When the situation deteriorated in 1955, the Army had to be called in. In June 1956, Phizo's Homeguards (as the armed division was known) used machine guns and rifles to attack camps of the Assam Rifles; they killed forty citizens and policemen on the Kohima-Imphal highway. Before a ceasefire between the Nagas and the Indian Army was declared in 1964, aircraft were used to bomb villages and the Nagas even brought a plane down using rifles. After the Army came in 1955, Zapu Phizo was smuggled out of Khonoma in a coffin and reached East Pakistan and, from there, using a fake Peru passport, he reached London from where he could not come back home. In 1990, his mortal remains came to Kohima in a coffin.

In 1966, Phizo sent his principal aide Thuingaleng Muivah to seek the support of the Kachin Independence Army—then fighting a dictatorship in Burma—and, ahead on that same route, the Chinese government. Adept at diplomacy, it was because of Muivah that both Pakistan and China have sustained Naga militancy. In 1975, Phizo's brother Kevi Yalie signed—with Phizo's concurrence—the Shillong Accord which made them irrelevant. In 1980, Muivah and Isak Chisi Swu declared Phizo a traitor and formed the National Socialist Council of Nagaland which is now known as the NSCN (Isak-Muivah), or NSCN (IM). Internal conflict within the NSCN (IM) that sprang from disagreements between tribes gave birth to the NSCN (Khaplang) which was led by S.S. Khaplang, a Naga from Burma. Naga militant organizations keep fighting amongst themselves even as they battle the Indian state. The saga of ceasefire, followed by peace talks, and undeclared war carries on. The problem, instead of resolving, has only become even more complicated.

~

To the left of the main gate which led into Khonoma was a grand church which the villagers had built out of stone with their own hands. To the right was an ancient morung, reached with difficulty after crossing many small alleys, where a young man was playing vintage pop songs on a cassette tape. The tape was worn through and only that young man could understand the lyrics. Outside the morung was an enormous drum that is used as an alarm in times of danger and to issue proclamations. The trunk of an ancient, huge tree is hollowed out and struck with clubs which makes it the approximation of a drum. There was also a dormitory with many old blankets and scores of wooden exercise clubs in the shape of pickaxes.

In traditional Naga culture, the morung is a nursery in which teenagers learn, among many other things, customs related to administration, traditions, responsibilities, communal activities, hunting and the use of weapons. During festivals, elders narrate the history of the village there. The morungs in villages used to be an exclusive space for the youth but the one in Khonoma was an exception. These morungs have rapidly vanished and now cannot be seen in most villages. There once used to be morungs exclusively for girls but have become extinct under the influence of Christian missionaries. In many villages, school-going girls have even stopped working in the fields.

The church tower standing in sharp relief against the blue sky was a symbol of Khonoma's pride. A service was underway in the giant hall. A priest sang hymns from a book. Murmuring piously, people kept their eyes shut and made the sign of the cross between the head and the breast. The children playing outside had had their hair combed. The women were in their best clothes, and some wore ornaments, but their dry, tangled hair and rough hands clearly demonstrated a hard life. Just as it was with the men, it was impossible to discern any emotion in the eyes of the women. The arms of Jesus Christ hanging from the cross were heavily muscled, like a weightlifter's; his beard was straggly and his jaw square. As we exited the church in the final moments of the service I asked Shashwat, 'Isn't their Jesus Christ strange?'

He held both his hands aloft and said, 'But Christian… Hulloluiah!' meaning he could look like anything but is, in sum, Christian.

A young man standing nearby and listening to our conversation came up to us and said in English, 'Our Christ is Naga. He was born here.'

The Nagas have adapted both the Church and Leftist thought and made them their own. The NSCN (IM) is Maoist in its ideology but its stated aim is 'Christian Socialism'. Their charter warns people about the deleterious effects of India (Hinduism) and Burma (Buddhism) and says: 'The forces of Hindutva... the Army, petty merchants, teachers, Hindi film songs, the makers of rasgulla sweets and the *Gita*... All these are the means using which our Christian God is being chased off the face of the earth.'

Phizo's house was just as it should have been. On top of it were two ancient crossed spears between which hung a rotting mithun skull. The roof was made out of wood and spiders had woven webs between the joints. Phizo had become a British citizen many years earlier. His son and daughter had tried to control the Naga national movement by remote control—just as Phizo had—but had failed and remained in London. They did not possess Phizo's resolve or his ability to chart new courses. Years before Phizo formed the NNC and picked up arms, he had set up a factory in a place as remote as Kohima to cold-retread old lorry tyres.

Once the highway between Imphal and Dimapur was built—when the British were still ruling the country—lorries began to ply and Phizo, who was then a Matric-failed youth, took a loan from two seths in Kohima at an interest of 150 per cent and set up his small factory there. The Muslim workers who were specialists in retreading lived in Dimapur and Imphal and Phizo could not convince them to relocate to Kohima. The lorries would not halt long in Kohima anyway and the factory folded. The seths filed a suit in the court of the British deputy commissioner,

Charles Pawsey, to recover the money. Phizo was poor and did not have the means to cover even the interest on the loan. According to traditional Naga law, a defaulter is cast out from his village. Phizo was exiled to Rangoon, under orders from Charles Pawsey, where he faced a great deal of hardship.

An elderly man named Sebi stood on the verandah of Phizo's house. He said, 'The Nagas still want a sovereign state but are currently going through dark times. They are divided amongst themselves.'

~

Khrini had built a new cottage after marriage and wanted to show off. The property, set among green alder trees, had a small gate and, across it, was a small lawn with a fig tree which had been brought from Jerusalem. At the door was Khrini's gigantic wife before whom he seemed a child. The fig tree, drenched in morning dew, declared that this house had been anointed with it; it was looked after better than all the other plants and people came to touch it.

The living-room walls were like a mischievous child's picture book but the decorations were traumatic. Numerous insects—butterflies, caterpillars, spiders, beetles, moths and cicadas—had been tacked on to the wooden walls only two days earlier and were drying post-mortem. The perpetrator of this artistic feat, Khrini, was standing in the middle of the living room and looking on at us with great curiosity. Since we Indians had come from the big cities, he was certain that our aesthetics would be commensurately well developed. He expected at least one of us to comment on his artistic interest.

Shashwat's eyes were glued to the butterflies which were the size of books. He said to himself, 'There was no need to decorate with these, they could have been eaten instead.'

As Khrini told us where each insect had been caught, his vast wife, who was making tea in the kitchen, laughed boomingly. She didn't know our language but could guess the state of our minds.

Like other Nagas, the residents of Khonoma refer to people from outside the Northeast as 'you Indian people' when talking to them. They know, from a very special sort of political awareness and sense of history, the shock which these words are capable of inflicting. If the listener has a picture of the nation in his mind, he must be practised in the art of leaving an empty space on the Indian map for these three words. They told us that each house in the village gives its boys to guerilla fighter squads on a rotating quota system and no resident from the area had ever joined the Army.

~

A small triangular cubicle. Soot-blackened maize cobs still in their swaddling sheaves hung from the ceiling like chandeliers. A bulb was suspended from a cobweb-festooned wire; its dim light fell on the bundles, boxes, clothes and farm implements strewn about on the wooden floor. A window, the size of a child's writing-slate; through the window, terraced fields and distant mountains could be seen. Sitting under the tiny, circumscribed world let inside the room by the window, an old woman—her eyes clouded by cataract—sat for a long time holding her son's hand and crying. Her grandchildren, standing around enmeshed with each other in a group, stared slack-jawed: Who was this stranger for whom their grandmother felt such maternal love? There was something primitive and pure about the woman's firm grip which had brought Chandola here from Joshimath after sixteen years.

This old lady who had once participated in the Khonoma wars and was now unable to move about much, was Harish's dharm-mother, a filial relationship consecrated by god and tribe and beyond the mere ties of blood. The window had been sawed out of the wall opposite her bed. Chandola could speak Nagamese—a patois cobbled together with Assamese and Naga words—but not Angami. She understood no tongue other than that of her tribe, but the two were easily sharing with each other their joys and griefs. They were outside the geographical boundaries of India and Nagaland, in a space where meanings drift off words like vapour and become sympathy, love and teardrops.

'Reto mei, reto mei.' (I'll come again... I'll keep visiting now.)

Harishchandra Chandola was born 3,000 kilometres from here, in Garhwal. He had come to Kohima as a reporter for *The Times of India*. Prime Minister Lalbahadur Shastri had got Harishchandra to resign from his job and made him his representative in Kohima. He was a mediator between the Nagas and the Centre even during Indira Gandhi's tenure as prime minister when the governor Braj Kumar Nehru became vexed with him and ordered him out of Nagaland.

Braj Kumar was the grandson of Motilal Nehru's elder brother and the prime minister's brother—Brother Bijju to her—who had come to help his sister, after having gotten time off from his job with the United Nations. In their respective memoirs, Nehru and Chandola have both remembered each other with a great deal of sarcasm.

The incident which finally vexed Brother Bijju provides a picture of the chessboard spread out between a government, an aware citizen, and the tribals.

A representative council of Naga leaders was in talks with the governor on 20 April 1968. Commenting on the issue of the Nagas acquiring weapons from China, Braj Kumar Nehru said, 'The Nagas are suffering from the "lemming complex".'

The Naga leaders did not understand what Nehru had said. One among them came out of the room where the talks were being held to ask Harishchandra Chandola what this 'lemming complex' was. The lemming is a rat-like creature found in North America, a rodent which commits suicide in hordes by drowning when their numbers increase beyond the supporting capacity of their environment. In a while, when Nehru got up to leave the talks, the Nagas accused him of violating the ceasefire agreements and boycotted the dialogue. Officers reported to the angry governor that one of the Nagas had come out of the room to speak to Chandola; it must have been he who had misguided the Nagas. In Chandola's next meeting with the prime minister in Delhi, she told him that he was not to go to Nagaland; Brother Bijju didn't want to see him there. Chandola still went to Kohima.

One day, eleven people from Khonoma landed up at his doorstep with a black rooster. One among them, Dirhe, proposed that Chandola be adopted as a son by Gokeso. A house would be built for Chandola and a rice field allotted to him. Were he to become a resident of Khonoma, they believed, no one could ask him to leave Nagaland. The eldest in the group, Gokeso, immediately wrung the rooster's neck and swung it five times around Chandola's head. The rest bore witness and as a mark of acceptance chanted 'ho ho ho!' thrice. He has since been Gokeso Mayasachu's son. That same night Chandola was arrested on the governor's orders. In the morning, the residents of Khonoma, armed with daos and spears, surrounded the thana where he was being held.

Brother Bijju was an elite among elites. When his own uncle, Jawaharlal, could not understand Braj Kumar Nehru's super-sophisticated ways, what chance did the poor, primitive Nagas have at conducting a dialogue with the man? He writes in his autobiography, which he had crafted specially for a European audience: 'Once, my uncle Biharilal Nehru was forced to wear a khaddar dhoti to bed in Anand Bhawan. When he woke up the following morning he found that his thighs had been scratched bloody by the coarse fabric.'

What should have happened, had things taken their natural course, is that Chandola, who once had access to the corridors of power through Nagaland, should have magisterially rested his hand against a pillar, or on a chair, and declaimed at length on militancy, the Naga question, the Northeast itself—a peerless expert on the region. But this did not happen. There must have been something fiery in his personality and in his journalism because of which he remained unpopular with officers and governors alike. For thirty years he kept tripping up the officers who came to Kohima claiming to have found the solution to the Naga problem but who were actually enjoying an extended picnic there.

A football match was taking place in a broad lane. Many of the players were wearing football boots but no one was allowed to play shots in that circumscribed space. Only short passes, dribbling, crosses and headers were allowed. Such was the speed and the unimaginable ways of getting the ball through that the game had been transformed into a powerful dance. Entranced, we sat down on an embankment to watch. The ball rose in the air and my eyes followed it. I saw a large hunk of meat hanging from a ceiling. There were different kinds of meat in that hunk which had all been hung from a sturdy metal hook fixed into a ceiling. Such hunks of meat were hanging from many of the ceilings of the houses there. I was surprised that having wandered about the village all morning, I had seen the meat only now. An electric thought came to me: Anybody could say anything, but the story which the barber from Dimapur had told me was true.

Evening had fallen. The footballers, shirtless and drenched in sweat, were on their way home. We too left for Kohima. Harishchandra Chandola's relatives had packed lots of food for us.

~

Visema village. It was impossible to believe that this old, cheerful, crinkly eyed woman standing in the premises of a house next to a gravelly street possessed such deep insights into Naga politics and had such an interest in the ceasefire.

She knew that journalists had come to the village and had sent her granddaughter Adi to summon us. At first sight she seemed like a simple rural woman who was drying paddy in her courtyard. She was mumbling continuously, and using a stick to threaten the hens which kept returning to peck at the grain.

She asked for three cane stools to be brought out for us to sit on, threw her cane aside, and stood straight. I had a camera in hand. She motioned me to stop and affectedly smoothed the wrinkles on her face with a palm, as if they would be magicked away and the lost years would come rushing back. Then she caressed her wrinkles with feigned wonder and made a face. She must have been a beautiful, proud woman in her youth. Her bilingual son, a teacher, took on the role of translator. It was only when she took a seat and directly addressed the Indian government and the Naga militants that we came to know she was Vizol's wife—Angami Vizol twice served as Nagaland's chief minister. The wrinkles underneath her eyes shone with self-confidence.

The sum total of what this cheerful woman, who was used to neutrally viewing war, bloodshed and conspiracies, had to say was that the Naga tribes should first stop fighting each other and present a united face to the world. Secondly, the Indian government should respect the Nagas's indomitable desire for freedom. God has created no solution to the Naga problem other than this.

'Among those newborns who had their umbilical cords cut with bamboo knives are many who are now doctors and deliver babies in hospital by Caesarean Section.' She set out this wondrous statement as the kernel of that truth which can explain the hearts of the Nagas. Changes of progress which took the rest of the world thousands of years to achieve had all taken place in Nagaland in the last eighty or ninety years. We have come from the Age of Head-Hunting straight to democracy, from divining rain through dreams to listening to weather reports on television. We have adopted these changes but are yet to internalize them. No one knows how much time that will take.

She was hinting at the sensitive nerve of the Nagas. The blind loyalty towards the village and the tribe often drenches Naga nationalism with blood, a nationalism which many Naga leaders, including Phizo, have tried to nurture but failed.

An armoury belonging to Phizo's federal government was looted by Sema Nagas. The split in the revolutionary army happened after a fight between the Sema and the Tangkhul tribes. When the NSCN split in 1967, the Sema and the Tangkhul went with Isak and Muivah while the Heimi and Konyak tribes sided with Khaplang. The Kuki are Nagas who are settled in Burma and Manipur, with whom bloody battles are waged. With Isak-Muivah are the Tangkhul, Sema and Phom tribes of the Zunheboto, Wokha, Ukhrul, Dimapur and Kohima districts. The Khaplang group has the support of Konyak and Ao tribes in Mokokchung, Tuensang and Mon regions as well as the Heimi Nagas of Burma. Both the groups have the most modern of weapons and internecine conflict aimed at the complete 'cleansing' of the other group is common.

The unbearable trauma of this indiscriminate bloodshed compels the spirits to descend upon some Naga individual from time to time and, under their influence, he appeals to everyone to forget the heads that have been severed and come together once more. This spirit-directed conclave is called the 'Shishi Ho Ho'. Most recently, the spirits rode an elder called Chosai of the Ketospomi village. The conclave went on for days and all the chiefs of all the tribes attended it, but no conclusion could be reached.

On the other hand is the Indian government which, according to Nagas in rural areas, is building a highway of currency notes from Delhi to Kohima. The aim is to utterly corrupt the Nagas and make them so dependent on luxuries and services that the thought of picking up the gun and going underground in the jungles just does not occur to them. This policy is showing results. Politicians and leaders, officers, contractors, middlemen and their families are all inordinately proud of their power and their 'easy money'. They have the same cars, clothes, scandals and rave parties which the nouveau riche youth of metropolitan cities do. The shine on their shoes and their cheeks contrasts vividly with that of the tough, shrewd boys of the villages. They all talk of shares, cricket, remixes, models and Facebook friends. They know everything about the most current fashion trends in cities and the latest dope being smoked there.

~

It was Christmas Day. A chill northerly was blowing in from Tibet over the Patkai Hills and into the valley. The entire village had been invited to a big feast in Vizol's house and we were guests there. It was sunny outside the church but the strong cold wind blew away the warmth. Girls were buying and selling Christmas cards. Many Naga men stood around wearing coats, stiff as scarecrows. Nagas from rural areas have a stubborn, wild simplicity about them which cannot be covered over by any garment. One can feel it in their grasp, and its emanation bothers one. During the service I felt as if the elderly men sitting in the back were expressing their keen disapproval of the young girls wearing jeans in a deep, low, murmuring growl.

It was in Visema that eight people had fascinatedly examined a mortar left behind after the Second World War and, in trying to fiddle with it, had been blown to little bits.

Vizol's house in Visema was built in the traditional Naga style and every corner was decorated with spears, matchlocks and wooden rifles. There was also a shoulder-high model of a light machine-gun carved out of a log of wood by an amateur carpenter which must have weighed at least 40 kilogrammes. As soon as we met, Vizol said in English, 'I am a free man now doing cultivation.'

In his view, Jayaprakash Narayan (JP) was the only Indian leader who understood the Naga problem at all. JP—along with the chief minister of Assam, Bimal Prasad Chaliha, and missionary Michael Scott—was part of the peace mission formed at the behest of the Church at the end of the late sixties. Vizol had a very poor opinion of those officials from Delhi who, pretending to solve the Naga problem, merely gave free rein to their prejudices and biases. He had himself fallen victim to them.

With no end to the violence in sight, Vizol had broken away from Phizo to form the United Democratic Front (UDF). The UDF intended to take the route of the

Legislative Assembly to present to the Centre the real problems which the Nagas were facing. In 1974, no one achieved majority in the sixty-seat Legislative Assembly. Then, seven independent MLAs joined Vizol's party and they went to the governor, Lallan Prasad Singh, to stake their claim. All preparations for the swearing-in of the new government had been made when the Home Ministry called. The governor was told that by allowing the UDF to form the government, he was nourishing a Bhasmasur—the raakshas who, after receiving a boon from Shiva, could turn anyone to ashes merely by touching him—because the UDF government would openly support militancy. The governor met Vizol alone and told him what Delhi wanted. Vizol tried to explain what would happen if instructions from Delhi were followed: The path of electoral politics which the moderate Nagas had adopted would be shut forever and the MLAs who had legitimately won elections and come to power would go underground into the jungles once more. The governor ignored the warnings from Delhi and swore in Vizol's government which didn't last even two weeks—power-brokers working for the Congress Party colluded with the Army to get some MLAs to defect. The MLAs who had defected were taken by helicopter to an Army camp and kept there.

Between this lengthy, informal interview carrying on in a homely atmosphere, with the shouts of children playing in the background, Vizol's granddaughter, Adi, who was an MBA student, asked, 'Will you have Christian curry?'

Shashwat and Harishchandra Chandola declined. I thought it must be some special Naga dish that I must taste. She immediately brought out a bowl with two large chunks of flesh drowned in curry. This mischievous girl's eyes had an emotion that was waiting in anticipation of something sensational, but I could not fathom it. The flesh was sweet and tough and I thought I had eaten it once before in Nagaland, but I couldn't be sure. She asked excitedly, 'Do you know what Christian curry is?'

When I shook my head, she said, 'Beef… This is beef. Cow meat.'

I could feel a reaction within me, a violent cyclone which could manifest itself as an explosion of rage, as tears, or as vomit. I had been trapped in a narrative as a character who would evoke laughter whenever it was mentioned. In the midst of pessimistic thoughts, a decision was made that I would not let myself be an object of laughter, come what may. But I didn't now what to do.

In embarrassment I closed my eyes and managed to say, 'Beef? Same as goat, same as monkey. Very nice little bit sweet.'

I had somehow managed to extinguish the firecracker of mischief which Adi had lit before it went off so I picked up the other piece from the bowl and ate it too.

In my dreams, my cow, the one with the long eyelashes, visited me. I used to take her out to graze. In my village, if a cow died of cold on a doorstep, her owner would have to carry her tether and roam all over the village begging for alms—atonement for the sin of cow-murder. Even today, if a cow is of an affectionate nature, she comes up and stands quietly touching me.

It wasn't the cow meat that I found indigestible, but the chasm between those who worship the cow and those who eat it.

~

General Thinusile seemed like those pehelwans who, in their youth, travel the world competing in wrestling bouts and gain fame but who, in their dotage, are utterly lonely. A cold easterly blows, joints ache—that is when they gaze into the past and find the energy necessary to pass time. This thought crept up to me via the dirty bandage which he had wrapped around his knee, one end of which was peeking out from underneath the hemline of his trouser leg. He lived in a crowded neighbourhood in Kohima village, in a small wooden house which, in view of earthquakes, had been built on stilts. Till as recently as two months earlier the general had been in hiding and the Army had been looking for him. It was only recently that the impression that he was with the NSCN had dissipated and it had been possible for us to meet him.

Two boys of indeterminable age and with identical faces came to Harishchandra Chandola. Dropping us off in front of Thinusile's house, they said, 'Go. The general's inside.'

Angami Thinusile Keho used to be a general in Phizo's guerilla army. But this was in 1971, when the Indian Army had arrested him in Bangladesh during the war with Pakistan. He shared with us memories of those days when he used to be a brigadier and how he, and 300 young Naga men, had marched 1,000 kilometres through the fearsome forests of Burma to China and carried back arms and ammunition. The Naga militants call that expedition the 'Great Long March'.

It began with a letter. The prime minister of Phizo's Federal Government of Nagaland, Scato Swu, wrote to the premier of the Chinese Republic, bringing militancy in the Northeast to international attention. His letter also ensured that the militancy—which was already being supported by India's enemy, Pakistan—received aid from China. Swu wrote: 'Without the aid of your great and powerful nation, the Nagas will no longer be able to battle India. The Nagas turn to you with hope-filled eyes to ensure the sovereignty of our land.' The two leaders who made up the envoy to China were Thinusile and the all-powerful ambassador, T. Muivah.

The expedition set out one morning from the dense forests of Khonsa in Arunachal Pradesh. China was in throes of its Cultural Revolution. There was no direct flight to the country. Not even with a connecting flight via Singapore the way it is today. Thinusile told us that the overland route through virgin forest was the only possibility. A jungle which no guerilla squad in history had ever crossed.

Thinusile was a past master at the art of extracting maximum results from minimum resources. In the dim light of the lamp he created a unique, unrivalled map of the landscape of the Burmese jungles on the back of his hands. On the thumbs and forefingers were hills; between the fingers ran rivers; his popping veins were trails; and at the sound of his feet beating upon the decrepit wooden floor, wild animals came bounding up, as did armed fighters from the resident tribes of the forest and sentries of the Burmese Army. As we bent over his gnarled hands, we looked through a pair of invisible binoculars into history and saw the Nagas wander in impenetrable jungles, toting guns, tents and provisions. They were speaking the state language of Nagaland, broken English, which merged with Nagamese, the sounds of wild animals, and a smattering of Hindi to achieve a lethal expression.

Thinusiles's utterances were not merely the words of a guerilla who had spent time in the jungles; it was his lived experience, an organic, biological impulse that was coming back to life. Rivers began to shimmer in the dark corners of the room which swelled at night to wash away a Naga asleep in his tent on the bank. Leeches flickered in lamplight and had to be battled every inch of the way across squelchy marshes. The spider webs stretched on the ceiling overhead were festooned with those crickets and ants which could swallow entire parties of men. In the frustration on Thinusile's face was etched the incomprehensible tongues of the Burmese tribes because of which they were forced to ford the same river thrice and each hill—so near on the horizon—took days to cross. Rain poured in torrents in the moonlight and there was no choice but to lie down on the ground in complete surrender like frogs and submit to its onslaught. The mysterious darkness of night surrounded them from all sides in those four months and made it impossible for them to distinguish between man and tree trunk. A scouting party of Naga hunters had been sent months in advance to find a path through the jungles of Kachin state, but that had been of no special help.

'If we weren't used to eating just about everything to survive, no Naga could have reached China.' Thinusile thus unveiled to us the mystery because of which Naga militancy is called the mother of all the militancies in the Northeast.

Militancy is an industry today. All Naga militant groups

provide weapons and instruction in the art of jungle warfare to nascent groups for a fee. A large part of these fees are made up of tax impositions, extortion through kidnapping, drug trade and smuggling. The other secret was strategic alliances. The men trekking to China had been saved from capture at the hands of the Burmese army, in their respective territories, by the Burmese Nagas of the Eastern Naga Revolutionary Council and the soldiers of the Kachin Independence Army (which was itself waging war against the Burmese army). On their way back from China the men had to repay the favours with some of the arms and ammunition they were carrying back.

The Nagas, posed as enemies of India, were welcomed in the Yenan province of China with the prestige as befitted exemplars of 'Communist Internationalism'. Muivah and Thinusile were taken to Peking. There they met the leaders of the Kachin Independence Army as well as those of the many militancies in neighbouring countries who were there, like they were, for arms and training. After a tour of those Chinese cities which are advertisements for the country's power and progress, the Nagas's training began in Yenan. The instructors tried everything in their power to lecture the students—apart from the coarser and finer points of guerilla warfare—on the ideology of Chairman Mao, dialectical materialism, peasant revolution, classless society, etcetera. On their part, the Nagas were surprised that the Chinese didn't have a god. Later, Muivah travelled to North Korea and North Vietnam to meet the Communist leaders there. He returned from these places with a 'packaged programme' comprising training in the art of conducting raids, organizing attacks, building a network of local spies along with guerrilla warfare.

The other end of the thread of this story was with Harishchandra Chandola who, at that time, was in Delhi to extend the duration of the ceasefire as part of his duties as liaison and peacekeeper between the Nagas and the Indian government. On the day Chandola met Prime Minister Indira Gandhi, she was busy with Cabinet meetings and was scheduled to fly to Moscow the following morning. Gandhi instructed Chandola that he should brief Sushital Banerjee, the joint secretary and the in-charge of the Prime Minister's Office, about the important points regarding the Naga issue. Chandola reported to Banerjee that, in response to the threat of deploying the Indian Army, the Nagas were trekking to China to acquire weapons and were trying to enter the Yenan province of China through Kachin territory in Burma. Banerjee summoned K.N. Prasad, joint director of the Intelligence Bureau (IB) and in-charge of security matters related to the Northeast. Chandola told Prasad that, this time, the Nagas were going to China instead of East Pakistan for arms.

Prasad said, 'They can try as much as they want, even their fathers cannot enter China through Kachin.'

'Why?'

'Because the Kachins are fundamentalist Christians and sworn enemies of the Communists. There are many hundred soldiers in the area, deserters from the Kuomintang era, who maintain large bases. They smuggle opium, heroin, jade into other countries through Thailand. The CIA airdrops food and arms for these rebels who are fighting China. They won't allow the Nagas to enter China through their territory. And if they do make it, the weapons will be taken from them on the way back. They cannot even dream of bringing in arms that way.' This was Prasad's personal analysis.

Thinusile, on the other hand, did not lose a single weapon or any member of his party on the journey. The first group of 147 Nagas came back in 1969, each carrying a cache of arms on his back. That year in June, a battalion of the Indian Army battalion stationed in Zakhama spotted a new Naga camp on the bank of the Zana river which skirts the Zhapu hill. The Army attacked, the Nagas returned fire and fled. But one Naga man was wounded and, in fleeing, left his semi-automatic rifle and some grenades behind. Some papers and diaries were also recovered from the camp. The following day, all the newspapers carried this headline along with a photograph of the lone rifle and the few grenades: 'The Army Attacks Naga Insurgents, Weapons Smuggled from China Recovered'.

~

Any conversation in Naga villages would start from the present and quickly veer off into oral history, folk stories and myths. At every step were wars, bloody stories of Naga bravery and in all minds were immense signboards upon which was emblazoned: 'We are an independent people, no one could ever rule over us.' I wanted to shout with the same intensity, the same passion: 'But what did you do with that freedom? Of what use was it to your society?' But these were useless questions because the Naga common man has no dreams for the future, and no hope. Not just at the level of the community, but at the levels of the family and the individual as well. For them the future is fluid time, unquantifiable. As easily as the Nagas exit the village and enter the forests, so will their coming generations slip into the future.

The last military campaign against head-hunting was mounted by the British in 1936 in the Pangsa village of Mokokchung district. The deputy commissioner of the Naga Hills, James Phillip Mills, and Major Williams mounted an expedition with 150 Gorkha soldiers and 350 coolies to carry powder and ammunition. Christoph von Fürer-Haimendorf, an anthropologist with London University, was also with them. The Nagas of Pangsa used to raid far and wide, reaching even into the villages of Burma to bring back the heads of men, women and children. They would capture other Nagas and non-Nagas, trade them as slaves, and would even bury them alive in cultivated fields to ensure good harvests. But the masters of the machete, the spear, and the fearsome art of head-hunting were forced to surrender in the face of powder and ball. Many prisoners, including a youn girl, were freed.

The Second World War broke out in a few years. A massive Japanese force swept over northern China and stomped over Southeast Asia, pushing the British out as they marched, and reached Kohima in March 1944. A few battalions of the Azad Hind Fauj commanded by Netaji Subhas Chandra Bose accompanied the Japanese. The Japanese intended to capture Dimapur and enter the Brahmaputra Valley. Dimapur, the first Indian railway station, was of strategic importance; the American and British forces fighting in South East China and Northern Burma depended on this centre for provisions as well as for arms and ammunition. Goods trains were carrying, on an average, 4,000 tonnes of supplies per day and storing them in Dimapur.

Most people in India have heard of the Second World War. The Nagas have suffered it. Aircraft propellers, tank parts, rifles, iron cannons, bomb casings—all of these can be found in houses in Naga villages, carelessly displayed like trophies. The Japanese lost because of the lack of foresight on the part of two of their top men: their chief of army General Kawabe and the supreme commander of the forces in South Asia, Count Terauchi. These two stopped their army from capturing Kohima when the commander of the 31st Division, Kotoku Sato, had even cut off the Kohima-Dimapur highway. The intensely fought Battle of Kohima, which is now part of the syllabi in military schools the world over, lasted over three months and was fought across an area of fifty square miles. The Naga elders describe how the entire hill on which the bungalow of the deputy commissioner now stands (next to which is a war cemetery) used to be clouded over by flies. It was strewn with the corpses of Japanese, Indian and British soldiers.

After Independence, the campaigns of the Indian Army began which the Nagas resisted with weapons left over from the Second World War and then with weapons they received from Pakistan and China. They also placed explosives in trains outside Nagaland and killed many innocents. Hostilities and bloodshed haven't stopped even after two ceasefires. Even without external aggression, war constantly breaks out between militant factions or between tribes; massacres are common, as is the razing of entire villages. In between all this, elections come around; corrupt politicians sponsor massive events (elaborate feasts) as well as bloody skirmishes with rival parties. Inter-party rivalries are long-drawn-out affairs. It is a fact that within recorded history, the Nagas haven't lived peacefully, either amongst themselves or with neighbours.

Prolonged warfare and brutality is spawning diseased, disillusioned generations. Many studies have been conducted on the Naga psyche, all of which point to two problems: apathy and madness. Terrorized children suffer from inability to concentrate and cannot learn anything in schools. Youth are prey to illusion, indignation and lack of empathy. The unstable adults remain tangled up in trauma and nameless fears. It is said that in all of Nagaland, people suffering from PTSD (Post-Traumatic Stress Disorder) number up to 50 per cent of the population.

~

The windows of the two-storey building adjacent to the Kohima Bus Stand—glorified by the appellation of hotel—in which we were staying opened out to the street and to the contemporary, 'non-official' reality of Nagaland. After darkness fell, a delirious siren would go off; a long, keening solo of uncontrolled indignation and directionlessness which meant: 'The boys are on the streets.' The windows would start shutting.

At different times of the night, three different gangs would walk on the street outside the window. Grown-up boys would sit in a circle, sharing a reefer and stopping every car with a non-Nagaland number plate to extort cash. Others would chase cheap, poor-quality brown sugar off cigarette-packet foils. The biggest group was a gang of teenagers who would lick Iodex and sniff petrol stolen from parked cars. They would shout in terrifying voices until late into the night, laugh and fight amongst themselves. It was quite common to see a frail, undernourished boy stop a stranger, snatch the cigarette from his mouth and demand 50 rupees.

The more experienced among the businessmen who come here step out of their hotels in Hawaii slippers and tear off their shirt-pockets. They fob addicts off with torn five-rupee notes. Salesmen working for private companies forget their lessons in grooming and become pragmatic—they keep their ties inside their pockets. NGOs use money provided by the government to paste bright anti-drugs and AIDS-awareness posters on walls. Every year, the anti-narcotics and police departments seize a few grammes of brown sugar, a few hundred proscribed pills, less than 300 litres of illegal hooch and are satisfied with a job well done. On every street one comes across boys, high on drugs, their eyes heavy-lidded, who cheerfully declare: 'The state government rules from space.'

There is one special variety in this new generation of Nagas who study in the expensive, exclusive schools of Shillong. In some cases the father, and, in some, both the parents of these children live either in the jungles of Burma or in camps on the Bangladesh border. These are the children of the members of the NSCN. The secret agents of the Centre keep an eye on these children in their schools and hostels. They tail relatives after school meetings and fill their diaries with jottings. The militants want to keep their wards in good schools in India, away from the jungles, so that their futures become secure. These children are their weakest points.

The Indian government and the NSCN (IM) have come to an unannounced agreement over the value of these boys and girls; under the terms of the agreement, the militant network is subject to a degree of surveillance while the children are granted an opportunity to fashion their lives and careers. Officials engaged with the insurgency make this claim with great confidence: After these young Naga children become used to a life of ease, receive good education and the assurance of a secure future, they will not go off into the jungles.

~

The rickety Nagaland Roadways bus with shattered windows reached Shillong at 3.48 a.m. We were stiff with cold and could not control our shivering; so hungry, that the thought of shredding the bus seats and eating them didn't seem funny at all. The passengers yawned long and loud, issuing primordial sounds from the back of their throats, and settled down with their mouths burrowed into blankets, sheets and folded arms. There were many who had travelled on those serpentine mountain roads with polythene bags into which they had vomited and hurled out of the windows into the valleys below. Above the pine trees dripping with mist glowered a black sky in which Venus was the lone glimmering star. We reached, but no one disembarked before sunrise. The reason why they didn't was much more compelling than mere cold. It was the fear of those Khasi boys, lying in wait to loot night travellers, which had seized every passenger.

Shillong is the preferred destination among the nouveau riche to educate their children, but the dropout rate among the local population of tribal students is high. Unemployment, alcoholism, drugs and AIDS are emerging as major social problems in Meghalaya. The jhum system of agriculture cannot ensure employment for all. The forests which are burnt down to create arable land become barren for years. And not everyone can get government jobs. There is intense competition among the tribes for reservation. The Khasi and Jaintia tribes receive 40 per cent reservation, combined, while the Garo tribe alone receives 40 per cent. The remaining 20 per cent is shared among the other tribes who live in the state. The Khasi Students' Union (KSU) is agitating for equal reservation for all. When their agitation heats up, the Garos begin their demand for a separate state. The Garos fear that if the quotas increase, educated Khasis will bag all available jobs. There is hardly any place in our country where there is no unemployment, but had these boys actually come together to form roving bands of looters, like the ancient Pindari thugs? I asked the conductor of the bus, a Naga, 'Will they really loot us?'

'Three days ago, at 6.30 in the morning, they took away everything from passengers, even their shoes and slippers. People walked home barefoot in the cold.' This was his short precis of a reply.

With the dregs of my hip flask and a badly rolled, lumpy cigarette for company, I spent an hour staring fixedly at the slaty-grey fog, fluffy like a puffed-up pigeon. During that wait, memories of those mornings of my childhood came crowding in when I would be the first one in the house to wake. It would feel then like it is time which is standing still, and man who is being spent.

Children started crying from hunger, wives began elbowing their husbands, and the opening strains of conjugal squabbles made themselves heard. We soon tired of the harsh sounds of clashing bangles and left for the guesthouse of the Baptist Church in Lachumiere, breathing clouds of vapour. It was locked. The chowkidar was asleep. His wife, a Nepali, said that the guesthouse staff would not arrive before 10 a.m. We left our stuff at the guesthouse and went out to explore Shillong. Not a single teashop was open for business. Dogs growled because the sheet I had wrapped around myself dragged on the ground.

In Shillong, the old capital of the Northeast situated 5,000 feet above sea level, the sun's first tender rays fall upon fruit-laden orange trees. Lakhs of glowing orange bulbs light up. A thin gold film falls upon churches, on pine trees, and on magnificent buildings constructed in the Anglo-Indian architectural style. Overnight, the fog had deposited a thin film of moisture on the rear windscreens of parked cars; the familiar crude symbols signs and the dirty phrases traced in the droplets by fingertips came alive in the light. When the emotions hidden among the phrases began to evaporate, someone came out onto the street and the day began. Gazing upon the beautiful Shillong laid out romantically as in a shop-window, we thought that we should rent a room in a local's house for a few days.

In front of the guesthouse of the Baptist Church was a middle-aged American man with a pair of scissors in the pocket of his trousers trying to thread a needle. A Bihari mattress-maker was seated in the lawn stuffing a quilt with cotton. The rust-coloured quilt was being stuffed for a Naga girl from Dimapur whom the American man had met via e-chat. He pulled out a pair of danglers from his pocket and, shaking them, declared, 'Jesus Christ has brought the two of us together via technology.'

'So this quilt is being stuffed in this cold for your wedding night, eh?'

The American was embarrassed. A bindi, a scarf, brassieres, a wedding ring... these articles, the raw materials out of which a global folksong was about to be composed, were stuffed in his pocket but we were not destined to stay in the guesthouse.

There was an unsettling cleanliness there, much display of the Bible, and a great deal of 'may I' and 'thank you'. The guesthouse would be locked after 7 p.m. and entry and exit were banned. In his previous life, the manager must have been the sort of man who is dubbed a strict landlord, the kind who looks upon his tenants' affairs as a king might view his subjects'. As soon as the thought of rebellion against this dictatorship cloaked in religion took root, the algae-covered roof of a white cottage further below on the slope gleamed. The house was a traditional earthquake-proof structure whose floors would quake and hum at every step. This building was a guesthouse for the Kendriya Hindi Sansthan and its director, Dr Pramod Kumar Sharma, took us home and fed us oranges, almonds and rasgullas. We could stay in one vast room at the rate of 15 rupees per day for as long as we liked. The design of the room seemed to have been inspired by the shapes which then lived in the innermost part of our hearts. The massive double bed stood propped up by bricks under one leg, the windows were slowly rotting, there were cobwebs on the ceiling and small gaps in the floor allowed us a view of the grass underneath the house. But of mattresses and quilts there was an excess. All at once we had become guests of the Ministry of Human Resource Development.

One downhill slope, then one more; about 250 steps from the guesthouse was a cottage identical to it. Venu, a forty-two-year-old bachelor from South India, maintained an office for a small English newspaper, the *Meghalaya Guardian*, in that cottage. Venu kept his hair in the style of Amitabh Bachchan in the superhit *Silsila* and tended it with great care. He lived in the office; he could be found sunning himself and drying his hair each morning in the lawn after a quick bath. A white handkerchief would be wrapped around his head to keep the locks from falling over on his face.

'Hello Benu how are you?'

'You yourself can see I am basking in sun.'

On meeting any one of the two of us, he would find opportunity to try his hand at Hindi grammar. And if we had an Assamese or a Khasi accompanying us, so much the better. He would relish each word: 'Paper in North India will write: Deceased was having sex. Arre bhai, if the subject of the sentence has died, and only his dead body is left, then how will any action happen?'

'What are you saying Benu? I've never heard of a man dying doing it.'

'Then another example: When shot was fired, the deceased was shitting. Hahaha…'

The most useful part of the *Meghalaya Guardian*'s office was not the newsroom but the small kitchen where we used to frequently find dinner—roti and vegetables. Of course, one had to endure Venu's short lectures on the glories of vegetarianism. By then all the hotels in Police Bazaar would be shut. It was more or less a rule that to keep ourselves from mixing drinks, one would carry one's quota along, a nip measure of Royal Stag whisky, which was Venu's favourite brand.

By 5 p.m., water droplets would condense on the windows. Someone or the other in the newsroom would get up, complaining about the cold and the bad weather and set about roasting papads which was the signal for each of us to wash our glasses and line up. Venu was excellent at rolling rotis; all we needed was for someone to quickly cook them. I made serious attempts to help a few times but this was a losing proposition. The rotis would be snatched right off the tawa and the one cooking them would have nothing left at the end. Even if some were left over there would be no vegetables to eat them with and they would have to be rolled up, dipped in whisky and eaten. It was pleasant, sitting in that cosy kitchen sucking whisky from warm, steaming rotis. Outside, in the darkness, an icy wind would be scratching away at the tin roof.

W.T. Jirwa, a tribal, and a photographer with the *North East Times*, was a frequent visitor. Jirwa always remained tip-top—our code for drunk. He was a Jaintia man who had had no formal education but was a master at the art of flirting with women. He was a man of principle: he would never accept more than a thousand rupees from the ministers whom he would ask for money. With that money, he would buy subsidized liquor from the excise department to distribute among his friends. Jirwa had a rare gift: after just three drinks he could say to any girl, any woman, 'You know, I love you' and give them love-hiccups.

He had many women friends. Following Jaintia custom, Jirwa would go to his wife's house only at night. There was also the young and handsome Suraj Joshi, a photographer, whose eyes blinked uncontrollably because of excessive drinking, who had married a 'ka kuddu' and who would tell us with pride how his father had migrated from Nepal as a labourer but had retired from the post of forest officer.

At times, Jirwa was an incomprehensible man. One night, he called the home of a reporter working in a news channel and said that the boy had been killed in a shootout between the police and the HNLC in Lachumiere. The reporter's mother, who had answered the phone, had to be taken to hospital. It was only when the son came to the *Meghalaya Guardian* office the following day and thrashed Jirwa that we knew of his mischief.

The most polished and the most news-rich reporter in that bunch was Frank whose brother was a minister in the state government. It seemed as if Frank had seen immense suffering but to talk about it would lower his dignity. Sympathy for Frank was an emotion that rose naturally. There were many women in the office who were romancing journalism at that time. A Mizo girl, Linda, and a Tripuri man, Sanat Chakraborty, lived in the cottage next door. They published a magazine called *Grassroots Options* with great zeal and amid tremendous paucity of resources. Anirban, who reported for *The Telegraph*, also lived next door. In this way, a small press enclave had settled during those days in lower Lachumiere.

Shashwat had found a new way to tease those beautiful girls, most of whom were Khasi. He would first allow them to fly their career-kite sky high and then say all at once,

'You should get married and serve your husband, have kids and rear them. Why are you giving your life to this thankless profession?' Then these girls and the other men would get together and have a go at Shashwat. In turn, he would be offended and ask me what I found so attractive in the babbling of those drunks when I, on the other hand, felt comfortable in their company. When Jirwa would be telling me tales of his flirtatious adventures, Shashwat would be lying upon a bench next to a lake near the Rajbhawan or in the guesthouse reading a novel.

'Everyone craves love but their ego keeps them from asking for it. I ask.'

'Women start loving you merely on hearing "I love you"?' I enquired.

'No. They loan me money, they feed me. If they are really tired of their husbands they might even love me for a week, a week-and-a-half. My advice is that every man should try his luck.'

'Even dkhars?'

'Dkhars take chances like mathematicians—the housewife in Delhi, a hill-station wife in Shillong. You see, if you marry a tribal girl you can get property.'

One day, I was sitting in the sun writing something when Yakku arrived, prancing. This street-smart Nepali boy, a regular Casanova, was a taxi-driver. I had assumed that he, like other jobless young Khasi men, would say, 'Eh dkhar, will you give ten rupee?' But he sat next to me and asked, 'Can't a driver become a writer?' This was the first pure, unmangled sentence in my language which I had heard in the Northeast.

Yakku knew so many secrets about the militancy, politics

and the nightlife of the town that nothing fazed him anymore. One thing which saddened him was the career of the call girls, which, because of drugs, he said, now began at fourteen and finished by the time they were twenty-one. Yakku was outspoken and carried himself with the swagger of a hoodlum. The press enclave of lower Lachumiere believed that he was an informer for the HNLC. He said one night, 'Our reporters are covered-rice eaters (jobless vagabonds who return home only late at night to find stale cold rice in covered pots). They report only what the government and the militants tell them to. Had I been a writer, I would write such things that the reader's eyes would fall out on to the paper.' Then, the bombshell: 'Does any reporter know that yellow cake (uranium) is available for sale in the underground market in Shillong?'

This sensational news could not be confirmed but the claim Yakku made wasn't entirely baseless. In 1994, 4 kilogrammes of semi-processed uranium, which a tribal smuggler had brought from the Atomic Energy Commission depot in Domiasiat, was seized in Shillong. The intelligence agencies had reported that this was done at the behest of a foreign agency or individual. A decade earlier, uranium ore was found in Domiasiat, 140 kilometres from Shillong, which is considered the largest uranium mine in India and which yields the very best quality of ore.

~

In every tribal language is a special equivalent for the word 'outsider'. The Khasi, who are of Mon-Khmer origin, call outsiders dkhar.

If a stranger is frequently seen walking on the streets of

Shillong, he is eventually asked if he plans to permanently settle in the state. Meghalaya—a Sanskrit word unfamiliar to tribals—was born in 1972 after a lengthy agitation against the imposition of Assamese, a dkhar language. The state has seen five large-scale anti-dkhar riots so far. Thirty-one lives were lost in the riot of 1992. Many Nepalis fled the pogrom of 1987 and reached Darjeeling and Siliguri where they provided the initial sparks to Subhash Ghising's agitation for a separate Gorkhaland. Despite the tribals' steady, organized opposition over a century and a half, more 45 per cent of the population in Shillong is made up of dkhars: Central government employees, Bengalis, Assamese, Nepalis, Marwaris and Biharis.

Khasi women are held to be the best at business in all of the Northeast yet, in Iewduh, also known as Bara Bazaar, the region's biggest Khasi centre of trade, the numbers of traders with non-Mongol faces is steadily on the rise. The language of trade is now Bihari-accented Hindi—'Ketna tthu pisa?' In the Iweduh, a sprawling bazaar spread over twelve acres and crisscrossed with narrow crowded passages, trade still remains in the hands of the Khasi women but whether it will remain so in future cannot be said. The ownership rights to the bazaar is with the Hima Mylliem and is managed by a committee of ten representatives. B. Nishan Wallang, a minister in the dorbar, was worried by the rise in the number of non-Khasis. Once an adviser fully endorsed by the king, Wallang had become a mere clerk due to the machinations of the autonomous council. He rued: 'Our ledgers show 75 per cent Khasi but on the ground more than 70 per cent of the shopkeepers in the Iewduh are dkhar.'

The Khasi have become used to easy money. They rent a stall from the dorbar for a pittance and sublet it to a dkhar for a fat monthly fee. The rent goes up every year, as do the number of non-tribal faces. The stall which fetches the dorbar 60 rupees per month brings the Khasi sub-letter 2,000 rupees—this is money earned sitting at home. The minister explained the economics to me: 'Annually, the dorbar earns 9 lakh from three thousand stalls. It earns an additional 13 lakh from smaller shops and petty traders. The dorbar employs thirty-six accountants, rent-collectors and chowkidars. Most of the rent is used to pay salaries to these people. Often, the raja himself doesn't receive his share and even has to pay out of his own pocket.'

Many intellectuals can be met in Shillong because the city is the academic hub of the Northeast. These intellectuals live in their own worlds. On being asked about changes in tribal society they cite a specific paragraph, not as if it was taken from an administrative report but from the Bible itself. This paragraph was written by the former chief secretary of Meghalaya, J.M. Phira (IAS), who was himself a Khasi.

> The tribal is straightforward, honest, trustworthy, hospitable and is also devoted to his family, his tribe and his community. His trust is shattered by the underhand means adopted by the dkhars. Tribals are often duped in matters of business and moneylending. Dkhars take over the tribals' land and their women. Numerous and long bitter experiences have made it a part of the simple tribals' character to view every dkhar with suspicion.

The Iewduh, which sells goods ranging from supari to software, is unique because it bears the deep stamp of a matrilineal society. The shopkeepers are all women and the youngest daughters maintain the books, for they will be the mistresses tomorrow. A pinch of Iewduh soil is necessary for the Nongkrem festival. The kwai-chewing women seated behind endless baskets of oranges, areca-nut, pineapples, vegetables and dried fish masterfully manage both their houses and their businesses. The meat market is so expansive that walking among the heaps of fat, innards and bones tires the feet.

Shillong is 150 years old; the market, even older. A century earlier, it used to be a weekly market, first in Nongkseh and then in Mwaitan. In British times the Khasi used to sell iron and potatoes to East Bengal and buy silk in exchange. In 1863, the British bought land on lease to make Shillong a cantonment and the capital of the Northeast. They also loaned money to the raja of the Hima Mylliem, Ron Sing Syiem, to modernize the Iewduh.

A narrow part of the Iewduh is called the 'underworld bazaar' where Chinese goods are sold. Carriers, most of whom are tribals, bring Chinese electronic goods into the city via Burma. These are cheaper than Indian brands and are hence much in demand. Bullets are frequently fired in this part of the market; both sellers and buyers are killed. According to the dorbar, the Khasis who intend to rent a stall in this part of the Iewduh bring no-objection certificates obtained by bribing the customs department so that smuggled goods can be easily sold. Each dkhar businessman must pay a tax to militants for which receipts are duly issued. These receipts are the traders' passport for Iewduh—and earth itself.

The tribal economy of Meghalaya received a massive

jolt in 1947, after Partition, from which it is yet to recover. Before Partition, life in the villages used to revolve around the weekly markets to which buyers and sellers from all the surrounding border areas, including Sylhet and Mymensingh, would come. The barter system was also very popular. Now this traditional system of trade has transformed into smuggling which works in collusion with the border security forces of the two countries. After efforts to stop the smuggling failed, a proposal to set up twenty-five trade posts on the border with Bangladesh was made, a proposal which has been languishing for years.

~

It was the fifth day of the new year. In the afternoon, Yakku looked out of the window of his taxi and shouted, 'Mr Writer, happy new year has happened in Dhankheti!' A little joy was also mixed in his voice.

The neighbourhood of Malki-Dhankheti was about 200 or 250 metres on the slope above, on the road which goes on to join the national highway. When we ran up, we saw police standing in front of Aristo, Shillong's largest store for electronic gadgets. An ambulance was about to carry away three corpses. A small crowd of people was peering in through the windows and seeing them for the last time. One of the dead bodies had a shock of curly hair which was wet—the man had been shot in the head. The shops nearby didn't shut down, no one seemed shocked, the police did not stop traffic, and no one was searched. The young Nepali boy who worked as a cleaner in Aristo was saying that that of the five boys of the HNLC who had shot up the store with AK-47s, two had been barefoot. Three store employees (two Bengalis, one Nepali), one customer and one kwai-vendor on the street outside had died. The customer, Jonas, was a student at Delhi University. Home for Christmas holidays, he had been buying a cellphone when the firing began.

On the other side of the police cordon the floor was sticky with blood. In the mess were a few red shoeprints, and the stench of gunpowder and charred flesh hung about the store. The employees were looking on at everything with stony eyes but were seeing nothing. The backrests of two chairs behind the counter were sieved with gunshots. One bullet had pierced the tinted window of the shop, exited on to the street outside where the kwai-vendor was. In one corner of a wicker chair, I came across a large quantity of congealed blood. This was where Jonas had fallen. Opposite the chair stood two new televisions with their backs to it; slivers of flesh were stuck to the perforations on the television-backs. There were two large pools of blood on the floor which had been covered by advertising banners.

Suraj, the photographer working for *Meghalaya Guardian*, was inside. When I shook hands with him I could feel him shiver. Shashwat tried to avoid the blood by climbing on to a pile of advertising banners but leapt backwards and stood gazing as if there were a deep pool in which he was drowning. Underneath the banners lay the body of the Nepali employee, which the ambulance was going to take to the mortuary on its next trip. The man's arms were strangely twisted, as if he had been trying to fly to avoid the bullets. A policeman started towards Shashwat who abruptly turned away and hurried out. Outside, the incident was steadily acquiring new versions. Some Khasi boys were saying, 'The rifles were shining in the sunlight and, before leaving, the assailants flashed a V for victory sign.' But it was an extremely cold day, blanketed with fog.

Gautam Bhattacharya, the owner of Aristo, who is counted among the ten richest businessmen in Shillong, was standing in a corner like a terrified child. Two years earlier, the HNLC had killed his younger brother in a similar incident. Upon his face was a slaty layer of ash. I repeated 'This is terrible!' three times before he responded in a faint voice, 'If the police hadn't meddled, three of my personnel and two customers wouldn't have been killed.'

This massacre hadn't been carried out to protest Indian imperialism, or to bring the demand for a separate state to the prime minister's notice. It had been done only—only!—to extort money.

The militants had sent a demand notice to store-owners before Christmas like they did in all the other years. As always, the police knew but, this time, for reasons unknown, they had decided to take action. Notices were recovered from thirteen such businessmen. The drunk young boy who was going around distributing the notices was arrested, beaten mercilessly and sent to jail. The police then sent news of the extortion, along with a list of the stores targeted, to newspapers and news channels. A CRPF company was stationed in Dhankheti for the protection of the storekeepers. The massacre had happened a day after the CRPF company had left.

At the press briefing that evening, the police superintendent of East Khasi Hills, G.H.P. Raju claimed that the police had information about the boys involved in the 'action'. He said: 'The faction of the HNLC headed by its chairman Julius Dorphang wants to extort without violence. This action is the handiwork of the more ambitious Bobby Marwein faction.' He also gave out the information that extorted money was being used by the militant leaders to add to their personal property. They have farmhouses in Ri Bhoi, he said, and coalmines in Lad Rymbai in Jaintia Hills. The militants lend money on interest to the very businesspeople from whom they extort, he claimed, and many big businessmen are themselves custodians of the militants' money.

The police superintendent had his eyes on the coincidence that two Khasi youth died that day in the action. He was using that delicate matter to play politics. If there was information about the murderers, what was being done to bring them to book? In reply, he made a politician's appeal: 'The Khasi community must itself decide if it wants to continue living alongside the snakes who have killed their own brothers.' The government's response to the massacre arrived that same evening: The HNLC may be a banned organization but the doors of dialogue still remain open.

While it is common for bullet-riddled bodies to be found on the streets of Shillong and for there to be no reaction to them, the atmosphere in town had completely changed by the following morning. Black flags flew atop houses in Dhankheti. At the church service after the slain Khasi youth were buried, the headman of the Malki area, H.P. Offlyn called the HNLC 'U Thlen' and demanded an explanation for the bloodbath. Two days later, eight women's organizations marched on the streets and demanded what it was that gave the HNLC a share of the people's hard-earned money. Speaking at a massive gathering, the women said, 'They are criminals and robbers; they should either surrender or prepare for consequences.'

The women also regretted an old incident in which they had supported the HNLC. The HNLC had held up an all-women branch of the State Bank of India. But, before the militants could vanish with the loot, the employees of the branch had demanded a song from the film *Kaho Na Pyar Hai*. The boys had all lined up like obedient children, sung the chorus from 'Kaho na pyar hai' and, saying 'bye bye sisters', had left.

The syiems also issued statements that they rejected the support of the HNLC in their struggle to have the monarchical system reinstated. The march of the women's organizations put the HNLC under pressure. It apologized for the deaths of the two Khasi boys but branded the three murdered dkhars as criminals whom they had been duty-bound to punish. In the following week, these words appeared on walls in the city: 'Don't simply talk about extortion, oppose it'. Then, a police outpost was attacked and four policemen were killed. Only two men dared to rise above the blind tribalism of that time.

Professor Almond D. Syiem of the North-Eastern Hill University (NEHU) said: 'This unrest after the death of two boys only proves that the Khasi listen to the voice of their conscience when it suits them and remain deaf to it when it does not.'

'The HNLC should come to the site of the massacre, to where blood was spilled, and try to separate the blood of the Khasi and the dkhar.' This said by Robert D. Lyngdoh, an MLA from Shillong.

At the office of the *Meghalaya Guardian*, Suraj was made fun of for having been scared. At the evening drinking session he was asked, 'Do you see, son, how it feels to be a dkhar in Meghalaya?'

Back in the guesthouse, Shashwat asked me, 'Tell me, why are we still here?'

I stayed silent. What his question actually meant was: Are we here to count corpses and be traumatized on a daily basis?

Abuse that had long been held back was on its way. The torrent would break upon me at any moment. Yet, abuse was better than silence.

I said, 'For a workout of our sensitivities.' But, instead of abusing me, Shashwat became grave.

The first militant organization of Meghalaya was set up for the purpose of extortion but it wound up after just two hold-ups. In 1989, Garo boys from the Goalpara district of Assam formed the Achik Liberation Matgrik Army (ALMA) to demand a separate Garo state. The NSCN (IM) trained these boys and outfitted them. The first raid was conducted on the Garo Hills branch of State Bank of India under supervision of the Naga militants. The ALMA never grew beyond thirty in number; this was revealed during the second raid on a branch of the United Commercial Bank in Mancachar on the Bangladesh border. An encounter with the police ensued; three Nagas and the self-appointed commander of the ALMA, George Momin, died. An enraged NSCN withdrew support, took back their arms, and ALMA was reduced to a ragtag band of hoodlums. Sixteen members of the ALMA, including its chairman Wilbur Sangma, were arrested. The ALMA wrote to the chief minister offering to surrender. A peace council comprising church elders and the Mothers' Union was set up, fifteen rounds of talks followed which were chiefly focused on reducing the quantum of sentences. Twenty-three militants, armed mainly with ordinary country-made weapons, surrendered on 25 October 1994. Seventeen were put on trial: each received five years in jail and a fine of 10,000 rupees for conspiracy to murder and extortion. A few hours after the sentencing, the governor announced a general pardon for all the accused and freed them from the jail sentence as well as the monetary fine.

The insurgency in Meghalaya is an import for which the citizens pay a back-breaking price. The NSCN maintains camps in Bangladesh and in the border villages of Meghalaya—which shares a long boundary with the country—have become transit points. The Nagas needed safehouses, guides, coolies and informers in Meghalaya so they built their own vast network in the state. According to secret reports, 75 per cent of what the HNLC makes through extortion is spent on buying weapons, on training-fees and fees for the supervisors of the 'action', all of which goes to the NSCN. If the perennial cycle of training and extortion was to end, the organizations on both sides of the border would crumble and scatter. Even politicians have been caught red-handed using these dangerous men—for a fee—during elections or to settle political scores.

The extent of extortionist militancy can be gauged from the far greater number of fake militants who have been arrested in the state compared to the number of actual militants. These fakes are mostly deserters from the Army and the police, or unemployed local youth armed with a few country-made weapons and a letterhead. Many such groups operate along the national highway and make their living off trucks carrying goods. A minister from Mawlang said, off the record, 'As long as the money keeps flowing, militancy isn't visible in Meghalaya. It is when money vanishes that bodies start appearing on the streets.'

A few nights after the massacre in Aristo I was half-asleep when I heard the four ancient mantras which had vanished soon after the beginning of our journeys in the Northeast. They were:

> William the sain sain
> Sain-a sain-a wa haré
> Churri
> Chur-kid

It must have been past midnight. The lamp was at half-light. Shashwat was pacing the room whispering these mantras one by one, a blanket wrapped around his shoulders. He would pace, stop to laugh, and pace again, chanting. This was an old trick which he would use to snap out of gloom and despondency. Whenever Shashwat would drown within himself, his mind, following preset strategy, would drag those incidents from the depths of his memories which would take him to completely opposite states of mind from those he was in, and cheer him up. This soul-struggle was an infallible technique of his but someone unfamiliar with it could ascribe it to madness. Shashwat's method was often successful but could be dangerous if it went on for too long.

These mantras had been born out of lengthy observations of two families in the Bairahana locality of Allahabad. Shashwat lived there when he was preparing to take the entrance examination for the civil services. The first family was secretive, and must have been experts at clandestine activities. The members of that family would always speak to each other in low voices. A third person listening in to their conversations might understand the sighing of the breeze but what they were saying to each other would remain incomprehensible to him. The head of that family had been given the name 'William the sain sain'— William the Whisperer. And so the entire family was quickly christened 'Sain-a Sain-a wa haré' in the typical Avadhi dialect of Allahabad. The head of another family in that same locality was a thin, dry, sucked-out sort of a man. Children would tease him with the name 'Churri'. His son, though well-fed and healthy, was fated to become the 'Chur-kid'.

I tried to distract Shashwat. 'This is why I say you should drink a peg or two before sleeping. See, take an average, the number of people dying at the hands of these terrorists in one year must be the same as those dying in traffic accidents in Delhi in one month.'

'But think, they had been alive only half an hour earlier. Showing calculators and mobiles to customers.'

Recreating the past was another of Shashwat's bad habits. Walking around ruins or historical sites, he would often stop. Stand still and ruminate. 'Imagine—this must have been the sitting area, that is where the hookah might have been placed, there the sentry would have stood, the children would play here, and there, all sorts of delicacies would be cooked.' He loved history, did Shashwat, but his nature was such that instead of learning lessons from the past he would try to transport himself there and live it.

'In the same way our bodies will lie, the world will trundle on.'

'Whose, yours or mine?'

'You sleep. Don't worry about me. I was only saying...'

The depressed bear crawled all over the walls once more. The bear's blood pressure might plunge. Or it might not. Who knew?

A cold wave swept Shillong. Our teeth chattered morning and night, fog hung heavy outside the windows even in the afternoon. Shashwat holed up inside the room and refused to go out. I would bring him lunch from Police Bazaar; the leftovers he would eat for dinner without bothering to heat up the food. Gradually, dinner started becoming morning trash. He would stay put in bed, propped up against four pillows, covered by two quilts and a blanket. His reason for not going out? 'No shoes.'

He would never wear shoes. He owned a pair of slippers which would somehow hold their original polish until they tore and broke down. When his feet became streaked with dirt, he would put on a very old pair of socks. He had stopped bathing when we were still in Nagaland. He had an old enmity with water. 'Your contempt for a bath is born out of your baseless overconfidence in your pretty face and your fair skin!' This statement would make him very happy. He would recollect incidents from his childhood when his fair complexion had gotten him a seat in a bus or saved him from a beating in class. He believed that the Aryans, first, and then the British colonialists have so conditioned our minds that even today a dark-complexioned man is considered untrustworthy while a fair-skinned one gives the impression that he is close to seats of power. He remained under the covers swimming, floating among the reminiscences of his childhood, the knots of history and his strange self-constructed beliefs. The light had to be kept on even in the daytime. I suspected that in my absence he stared at his palms.

Around this time Ratan, a clerk working with the Hindi Sansthan, began to visit the room when I wouldn't be there. Ratan was from Agra. He would tirelessly complain about how his superiors had avenged a sin from a previous life by transferring him to Shillong and how hellish life for the dkhars was. Sitting in the freezing gloom he would spill his cup of woe. Shashwat, his face dug into the covers, would listen and go 'hoon, hoon'.

'Ratan-babu, how are you?'

'Arre saab! Dying, but not talking about it.' This was his refrain.

One day, Yakku said to me, laughing, 'Mr Writer, your friend will be born in a sweet manufacturer's house in his next birth.'

'Why?'

'Whenever I go to your room to look for you he asks if I can tell him about a good sweet shop.'

'If you do, tell him.'

I understood that he had finally managed an appointment with his uncle, the governor of Assam. The following week he got Ratan to bring him two boxes of sweets, bathed, spruced himself up and left for Guwahati.

When he returned two days later he seemed very happy and was practising a fragment from a classical song.

> A fish got my ring.
> Someone go tell that younger devar of mine
> To have the Ganga trawled...
> That fish is mine.

This followed a pattern. If he was happy he would hum a fragment of a song with utter concentration all day or over many days. He would turn that one fragment this way and that and polish his every emotion with it. He would dive deep into music, the lives and times of singers, recipes, table manners at kingly feasts, the architecture of ancient monuments, the ways of the old nobility—their pride and their sophistication—and spend hours talking about these subjects. I would feel then that he was heading a delegation from ancient India to the modern profession of journalism and was looking for reasons why these ancient customs had become extinct in the first place.

One of the other signs of the good days—the Widow. The contradictions in Indira Gandhi. 'Widow' was the only word which he used to describe the ironies of the former prime minister's personal life and the contrary winds she faced in her political career. Shashwat's endless commentary was on the familial permutations and combinations of the Nehruvian era which had shaken Indira Gandhi into existence, that rare cocktail of feminine beauty and masculine politics.

He stayed up till late at night, that darling little prince of a nephew, describing how happy his aunt had been to see him. She said, 'Munna, now you're of age, have yourself anointed with turmeric, get married.' She had all of Guwahati scoured for dal-pakoras, made a curry out of them with her own hands and, smearing ghee on hot rotis, fed him. This was a childhood favourite. She remembered…imagine! We kept talking of food, of festivals, long-forgotten relatives… There such ease, such laughter!

'*You* would think it indulgence! This scoundrel laughs while Assam burns, you would say. You are more jealous than a barnyard cock… You would fling a bone into a vegetarian kitchen. So I didn't take you along.'

He sat there and grew smaller and smaller—a thirty-five-year-old who shrank into a portrait of a baby.

'Did you talk to His Excellency about our trip?'

'He wasn't there. And… was this a worthy topic? Should I have said: We are vagabonds living hand to mouth? I told my aunt: I had come to offer my respects, now I'm leaving.'

The following day was sunny and lakhs of orange bulbs were aglow. Shashwat proposed that Shillong should be properly seen. We took an overbridge to the right of Police Bazaar and walked past colony after colony of houses, engrossed in talk. Shashwat would occasionally stop and point at a house. 'Look, the dwelling of a refined, civilized man.' Two hours later we climbed down a steep slope and reached a densely populated locality, exceedingly filthy and poverty-stricken.

A big drain was flowing underneath a bridge. A bedraggled puppy was fighting for its life in the freezing water. A group of Khasi children lay in ambush on one side of the drain; each time the puppy would be ready to clamber out they would push it back in with a piece of wood. When the filth-smeared puppy would yowl in agony, the children would scream in excitement. A slit-eyed old man, leaning on the railing of the bridge above, was smiling, lost in this game. The children's joy rode up to him upon the whines of the dying puppy. This scene, the cruel future of the tribal communities, was what must have shocked Shashwat. He ran down to the drain. 'Hey… Hey… Let it go… Let it go… Why are you killing it?'

Even after Shashwat became gainfully employed he would regularly bring home a whelp off the streets each winter. They would all receive the same name: 'Lumdigdig'. The puppies' exploits would be conveyed to us with the same passion with which the blind poet Surdas wrote this line about the child Lord Krishna: 'At times he closes his eyes, at time his lips flutter.' Shashwat would play with the puppies, nose to wet nose; if they fell ill he would take the day off and look after them; if they died, he would mourn them.

The children paid him no attention. Shashwat looked up at the old man. The man said something to the children in their language and they ran off. The puppy, trembling and unsteady on its legs, followed.

Having walked some distance we came upon a general store. Its minder dozing inside. He asked, 'Are you outsiders… Get out, quick! The boys here are dangerous. Don't you know this is Mawlai?' Fear could be sensed in his voice.

Fifteen minutes later we were sitting in a teashop where a primary-school teacher gave us the lowdown. 'See, even the city folk fear Mawlai but cannot avoid it; the cemetery is here. Julius Dophrang's house is in Mawlai and most boys in the HNLC are from these parts. Guns go off the night before every anti-government agitation. Dkhars often turn up dead in the surrounding drains and forests. My relatives rarely visit; you see, music systems are lifted from parked cars. Gang wars take place. Local heroes spring up overnight and die overnight. And the police stay away.'

Before we could decide what to do next the schoolteacher hailed a taxi and practically pushed us in. We hadn't even finished our tea. He was a self-appointed public relations officer for Mawlai terror, that man. Back in the guesthouse Yakku said, 'No taxi-driver goes in Mawlai though his bladder may burst. His car will vanish as he pisses.'

Later, the traditional king of Shillong, Loborious Manik S. Syiem said to me, 'Mawlai is a different public but every city has its own Mawlai.'

On the way back Shashwat exclaimed, 'Savages!'

That night he looked for and found one more ancient mantra which went: 'Chala aao... Chala aao... Moseebat mein keu keu ke saath nahi dey-at'. (Come along... Come along... No one is yours in times of trouble.)

This mantra had been gifted to him in his childhood by his maternal uncle, Suraj Prakash Adeeb, former excise commissioner with the government of Uttar Pradesh.

'A goldsmith couple lived in our neighbourhood in Sultanpur—Sunaar and his wife, Sunaarin. Both were centenarians. Inside their house was a well. Sunaar would limp along slowly. Sunaarin had lost her voice and could only speak softly. After Sunaar went to bed his sons would oil his wooden slippers so that he might slip and fall into the well. Then they would get the gold, the business and the house. When he didn't, the sons began to give jaggery to the dogs so they would become tame. Both Sunaar and his wife woke up together one midnight; thinking it was morning the couple left for a walk. Their boys set the dogs upon them. Sunaarin ran off. Lame Sunaar said in a teary voice: 'Ruki jaao... Ruki jaao... Aao-at ahi.' (Hold up... Hold up... I'm coming.)

'Chala aao... Chala aao... Moseebat mein keu keu ke saath nahi dey-at,' Sunaarin said.

~

By six, the streets would be deserted. I went out one evening to make a phone call and found chaos. Cars were dashing about to and fro, their red-blue lights flashing, sirens blaring. A cloud of smoke rose from behind Governor's House and drifted up lazily to collect in the sky. Behind the smoke a reddish glow drifted and shimmered. A man in the PCO said that the HNLC had set fire to a dairy belonging to a Bihari in Mawlai. On my way back I met sweat-soaked Jirwa who had come to fetch his camera stand. He said that it was the Legislative Assembly building which was on fire; all of Shillong would soon burn.

I ran to the window of our room in the guesthouse and shouted, 'Let's go see, the Vidhan Sabha building is burning!'

'Eh... What's there to see?' A voice rose from within the pile of quilts. Shashwat was in no mood to stir.

'It is eighty years old, and from the British times. You've

seen the architecture… It'll be around only a few more hours now.'

'In this cold? Screw it… Old and new things burn the same.'

'It's a big fire. It'll keep you warm.'

Some local boys were racing to the scene. I sprinted after them.

Constructed during the British Raj in 1921, this building was one of the most important structures in the Northeast. It had served as the Legislative Assembly for undivided Assam earlier and now served Meghalaya. The roof had burned through and caved in because of which many among those gathered to watch were seeing the inside of the Assembly for the first time. The old wood was crackling; in the innermost parts, flames were leaping. Triangular arches, pillars, the treasury and the benches upon which the Opposition would sit, doors, windows—everything stood in their places, smouldering red as if the bright lights of Diwali had been wrapped around them. In front of the entrance was the flagpost. The flag had become ash as had its hoist-rope, but the latter remained wrapped around the pole. Almost all the photographers had set their machines on stands anticipating hours of shooting. The fire brigade was standing quite a distance away towards Police Bazaar—they were no longer called upon to extinguish the blaze but to prevent the surroundings from catching fire.

A large crowd had gathered to soak in the warmth coming off the Legislative Assembly. Cigarette- and kwai-vendors had arrived for business. People sat in small groups, drinking. One corner had been cordoned off by the police so that the chief minister, officers and MLAs could watch to their hearts' content. Even though this was a terrible fire, the people were happy that at least one symbol of the power of venal, corrupt politicians was burning in front of them. By dawn the heat became too much to bear and the spectators went back home. The morning papers were dripping with the laments of political leaders, architects, administrators and intellectuals. A former MLA from undivided Assam, by now an elderly man, said: 'It feels as if my own mother has been burned to death, the mother on whose lap I learnt the alphabet of politics.'

Anirban's story had been printed in *The Telegraph*, in which he had said, quoting an official, that the HNLC could have had a hand in burning down the Legislative Assembly building. A letter was found in the evening, printed on an HNLC letterhead—'The newspaper will apologize or the reporter will prepare for consequences'. The number of bottles consumed in the *Meghalaya Guardian* increased. Venu, the editor, pulled at the hair which fell over his ear and said to me, 'There's a dog in Shillong, write a story about it. When a horse-cart laden with oranges travels on road, the dog runs underneath. As soon as the oranges are unloaded, hup!, dog jumps up on cart. He looks around as if to say that it was me, see what a big load I pulled.'

This open sarcasm was directed at Anirban who was sitting nervously nibbling on a papad. An apology appeared in the *The Telegraph* the following day but a boy came to Anirban's room and asked him to leave Shillong if he valued his life. That day it felt as if all eyes in Shillong were upon Anirban. Wherever he went, tribals would whisper among themselves, 'This is him, the one from *The Telegraph*.' That evening he vanished. Colleagues said to each other,

'We will soon have to call a condolence meeting.' But I saw him the following Sunday; he had a little girl in his arms. He was coming back after having had polio drops administered to his two-year-old daughter.

In response to the threat Anirban had gone off to Guwahati to fetch his wife and daughter. In his own way he had sent a message to the HNLC that he wasn't afraid—if you want to kill me you will have to kill all of us. I congratulated him: 'If there is a little life still left in journalism, it is because of reporters such as you.' The fabulist father within him came to the fore. 'When I tell her the story of the lamb and the wolf, I will say: If the lamb flees, there is no riverbank in the world upon which the wolf will allow her to drink.'

~

If the body wastes away, if the skin loses its lustre, and a sharp pain frequently rises in the stomach, the Khasis say that U Thlen has got you. U Thlen is a snake which drinks human blood. Even today many Khasis believe that those who rear this snake still live in Sohra (the older name of Cherrapunjee which means the 'country of oranges').

This mythical snake wasn't always domestic. And how it came to be domesticated is a story in itself.

There was once a time when humans, spirits and the gods lived together. U Thlen lived at the far end of the world, in Sohra. U Thlen was a shapeshifter and could take any form but he preferred to be a massive snake with his snout in a cave in Pamdoloi and his tail dipping into a chasm in Lingkhrang. U Thlen was the grandson of the deity of Mawsmai, U Mawlang Syiem, and the son of his loose-charactered daughter, Ka Kama Khrai. She became a fallen goddess and was banished to Pamdoloi falls where she lived in a cave with her son. She decided that her son would be reared exclusively on human flesh. He would ambush people on the road to the Rangeth weekly market to the west of Sohra, and would catch and swallow the last person in every band of travellers. One of his victims was a trader from Sylhet. When people searching for him vanished too, the frightened Khasi people prayed to the protector of souls, Suitanoh. Suitanoh got the lyngdoh, the priest, to cast a massive iron ball and a pair of tongs. The deity then heated the ball until it was red-hot and, picking it up with the tongs, tossed it into U Thlen's mouth. The earth shook with the serpent's death throes, hills crumbled, and the sun was eclipsed by dust. Suitanoh summoned the people of Sohra and Sylhet and ordered them to dice U Thlen where he lay, cook his flesh and eat it but to beware: not one little piece of flesh should be left unconsumed. All of U Thlen was eaten save one piece which an old woman took home to her son. She stored the meat in a bamboo basket and forgot about it. After many days a snake emerged from the basket and told the woman that if she followed his orders, he would grant her untold wealth. The woman became greedy. The snake granted her immense wealth. One day, U Thlen said to her, 'I have made you rich. Now you must bring me a human to eat.' When she couldn't, U Thlen devoured her grandson. Terrified, the old woman hired men to fetch human blood for the snake. It is said that 'Nongshohnoh', the practice of keeping hired killers, began then. The woman's family taught many others the art of keeping U Thlen—an art many say is still in practice.

'What is the white man's age? Two monsoons.' Another saying that is famous in Sohra.

The tribals of Sohra have a name for torrential rain: 'Slaoop'. If torrential rain falls for nine days and nine nights it is called 'Daniew Miyat'; if for fourteen days and fourteen nights thick ropes of water tie heaven and earth it is called 'Khadsa Miyat'. People find shelter from the rain under tightly woven bamboo mats which cover them from head to heel. But when I reached Cherrapunjee I heard that, lately, an alien word has invaded the local vocabulary: drought. They say it rains so little in Sohra that locals make do with folding umbrellas.

A visitor to Cherrapunjee in the winter months, especially he who goes there with a pitter-patter impression of the place, receives a stiff jolt of surprise. When he enters this hilly area—which receives annual rainfall in the range of 10,000 to 12,000 mm—he will find small wheeled trolleys crawling on the road bearing empty canisters and drums. People range far and wide to fetch water and keep their households from becoming parched. The public taps installed by the public health and engineering department yield water only for ninety minutes a day. The one who manages to fill up in this time—either by industry or by trickery—smiles a winner's smile; the others set out to look for sources outside Sohra, empty vessels in tow. The causes of the decreasing rainfall are put down to deforestation, an exploding population and environmental imbalance, in that order. Some among the more well off have even begun to buy the precious fluid. Thirty rupees for 5 litres is the maximum charged so far.

The total population of Cherrapunjee used to be 4,000 thirty years earlier; more than 40,000 live here now. Indiscriminate tree-felling for jhum cultivation as well as for limestone- and coal-mining has denuded entire hillsides. In some areas, however, oak forests still remain. They survive not because of environmental considerations but due to the same fear which keeps even the bravest heart from pissing on temple walls. Two deities, U Ryngkew and U Basa make their homes in oak trees and the Khasi worship them. It is considered a crime to cut down oak trees for all purposes other than last rites.

A very desi strategy was used in the PHE office to fob off complainants. First, the officers explained that Cherrapunjee is built upon a limestone mountain which soaks up all the water. Next, he was made to stand in the sun for five minutes. He was then asked, 'Do you feel the steam rising up from the ground?' The man would nod yes and leave.

'Rathole-mining' is a cottage industry in Cherrapunjee. The miners do not employ any machinery; using only pickaxes and shovels they dig a ten-foot hole in the ground. Coal is then extracted from the horizontally extending tunnel until the roof collapses. The maximum number of mines are in the Jaintia and the Lad Rymbai areas. Broad estimates put the daily production of coal in Meghalaya at 18,000 tonnes, most of which is sold to Bangladesh. This trade runs with the collusion of local leaders, the mafia, contractors and transporters—who are often exporters—because, after the nationalization of coal and coal-mining, rathole-mining has been deemed illegal. The business is murder on the environment but puts cash in the hands of the locals and the state government has been consistently lobbying the Centre to keep rathole-mining outside the Nationalization Act.

Many unfamiliar aspects of monsoon are to be seen in Cherrapunjee. The Agent of the East India Company, David Scott, had set up headquarters here in the final days of the nineteenth century. But when young English officers began to commit suicide, the headquarters had to be shifted to Shillong. We found three graves in a lonely spot, covered over by vegetation and debris, upon which was graven in faded letters: 'Killed by His Own Hands'. The deafening, endlessly falling rain, the fog which hung heavy for months on end, the creeping mildew and damp had created such despair in their hearts that these men had chosen to shoot themselves.

We were to meet the king of Cherrapunjee, Freeman Singh Syiem. He was astride a bike, wearing sunglasses, and on his way to scout new sources of drinking water in the neighbourhood. He was happy that the maximum amount of rain in the world falls upon the land of which he was king and anxious about where to sell the bumper crop of twenty-seven different varieties of oranges which had been harvested that year. According to him, if the government did not allow trade with Sylhet, the local unemployed boys would form a militant organization and started extorting tourists.

In that town is a small museum, as also a mutth of the Ramakrishna Mission. Someone or the other invariably says that the record for maximum rainfall has slipped from Cherrapunjee; it has gone to Mawsynram. The mutth had so many dos and don'ts it seemed as if Vivekananda had gone away but had left behind officers of spirituality in his place as regulatory authorities. The museum is unique. The excessive rain and humidity allows nature to works its strange alchemy. It produces butterflies, moths and insects of the most vivid and fascinating varieties. Some come into existence in minutes and, just as soon, hand Cherrapunjee over to their next generation. Butterflies larger than elephant ears in span; insects in a mad riot of colours were on display in the showcases of the museum. It became clear in a flash where Khrini from Nagaland had found inspiration for his wall decorations.

Mawsynram had hundreds of dry waterfalls, some of which still carried thin runnels of water. The deep pools and fantastic shapes made by the water plunging into the valleys spoke eloquently of the mad power of these fast-flowing rivers. These water-horses gallop southwards over limestone slopes with such anarchic haste that, come monsoon, even locals gaze upon the transformed landscape and put their fingers between their teeth in wonder.

The final limit of Indian territory is the Giant Basket, a rock formation. Looking down 4,500 feet from the Giant Basket one sees green baubles strung upon silver wires and ants crawling between them. The silver wires are the rivers of Bangladesh. The green baubles are villages and towns between which the trucks that ply on the highway gleam.

Most of the water flowing from Cherrapunjee contributes to the annual floods of Bangladesh. Locals say about Dainthlen—the cave where the people of Sylhet and Sohra feasted off the flesh of U Thlen—that a woman can be heard weeping at a waterfall nearby. We tried very hard but could not hear her. One reason for this could have been that we had found nothing to eat since morning. We could pay attention to nothing because of hunger.

A party of Bengali tourists was eating lunch. Their guide was a short Khasi girl, an employee of the tourism department. We asked her, 'Can we get anything to eat around here?'

'Chuna fattar, chuna fattar,' she said with her hand raised and pointing towards Bangladesh. Indeed, we were surrounded by limestone mountains.

'What is your good name?'

'Britannia Esther Nongkren, sir.'

'Who are these people?'

'Chuna fattar, chuna fattar.'

She respectfully pulled out two almost transparent chips from the packet in her hand, gave one to me and the other to Shashwat. I thanked her and, comparing the weightless chip against the keenness of my hunger, asked, 'What is this?'

'Chuna fattar, chuna fattar,' Shashwat replied

~

The day after we returned from Cherrapunjee, 22 January, Shashwat left for Sultanpur. It was the fifty-fourth day of our trip.

His briefcase and sleeping bag were on top of the taxi, tied up alongside his co-passengers' luggage. He was in the front seat, applying Otrivin to his nostrils. That nasal drop which earlier had a home in his pockets was to be found more and more in his hands. The red jacket which he was wearing—the one I had gifted him at the beginning of the journey—was filthy. Its bright colour was now a mere memory. His face had changed too. His eyes had become alert and wary but the corners of his mouth drooped and so did his shoulders. He was to catch the evening train from Guwahati.

'Stay sharp in Manipur and Tripura, eh?'

The medicine was finally in his nostrils. He blinked, took the medicine-dropper held in his small hand and pointed to a hoarding with it. 'Don't go out drunk, okay?'

The hoarding was one of those advertisements posted by liquor prohibition departments that are visible all over India. Towards the top of the signboard were these words written in red: 'Children Will Starve Fathers Will Drink'. Underneath the words was the illustration of a bedraggled-looking man, holding a bottle in one hand and dragging a woman by the other. A wailing child followed the couple.

'If the child is not staying behind, the father can do whatever he wants. How does it matter?'

The taxi lurched forward; all at once Shashwat grew restless and patted his pockets. He didn't have a reservation on the train. He had to get his ticket confirmed once he reached Guwahati. I thought, Now is the time to fill up my flask with homebrew and ask truck-drivers for lifts.

In our room in the guesthouse was Shashwat's cave made out of quilts atop which were strewn huts made out of books lying face down, newspapers, empty medicine packets and biscuit wrappers, all of which were visible in the dim light of the lamp. To understand what he might have been thinking before he left, I entered the cave. I believe it is possible to gain access to a mental state by mimicking a pose or a posture and, conversely, to acquire a pose or a posture by mimicking a mental state. As a child

I was fond of imitating the facial expressions of grown-ups to guess their thoughts. And the thoughts which arose when carrying out these imitations, I would assume were true. I would often mimic chameleons, oxen, goats and dogs in solitude. This helped me because the uncertainty within me would vanish.

I slept until evening propped up against five pillows in the Shashwat Mudra.

After dark my slumber was broken by a song sung in a sweet lilting voice. It was strange that in so many days my attention had not been drawn to it. But it was also true that I hardly stayed in the room in the evenings. The man singing was Sangma, the chowkidar who lived in the lean-to next to the guesthouse. I lay in bed for a long time, listening to Sangma and his Achik folksongs, and finally fell asleep again. When I complimented Sangma for his song in the morning he became shy. But he then launched into another song, his voice pitched higher than it had been the previous night.

I would now conduct my evening drinking sessions in his company and find myself feeling like a wonder-struck shepherd lost among the mountains.

~

There was a curfew-like silence in the evening before 26 January, Republic Day. The HNLC had called for an all-Meghalaya bandh lasting thirty-six hours. Only CRPF and Army trucks could be seen on the streets, in the front of which were machine-gun barrels sticking up. The director of the Hindi Sansthan, Pramod Kumar Sharma, extended me an invitation: 'Don't go anywhere before 9 tomorrow morning; a Republic Day ceremony has been organized.'

On the morning of Republic Day, Sangma took me to a room where four or five gloomy-faced officials were gathered. All at once three tension-filled minutes arrived. The curtains were tugged at to see that they were securely shut, the door was bolted with care. A flag was brought out and placed on a table in the room. Everyone got up. The flag was taken away and plates of biscuits and savouries were placed on the table. Everyone began sipping tea, the relief of having discharged a serious duty writ large on their faces.

On Republic Day the governor had invited sixty former freedom fighters to a flag-hoisting ceremony. Two attended. Four sent their relatives. Ratan-babu told us: 'Nation-worship has seen 100 per cent increase because last year only one freedom fighter came to the Governor House.'

Twelve militant organizations from all over the Northeast had called for an eighteen-hour bandh. Fifty thousand troops of various Central government forces remained on high alert. Even in a small, relatively peaceful state such as Meghalaya, three extra BSF companies had been deployed—BSF because the CRPF was largely deployed in Jammu and Kashmir at that time. All government offices observed Republic Day in the same way: behind closed doors. Television programmes showed chief ministers and governors of all the states of the Northeast saluting the flag and addressing unoccupied chairs, stray dogs and the four terrified corners of the compass.

~

In the new year, Shillong became picture-postcard pretty even though the cold was excessive. I was mostly in the company of Yakku, emptying bottles and making the rounds of the bachelors' quarters, but boredom had set in. I would get angry with the cold for everything. Sangma had left for home on holiday.

Then, one evening, I saw a ghostly shadow in the dim light of the lamp.

'Manisha Koirala is coming for a musical night to Lad Rymbai.'

'So!'

'She has the same eyes as the women here which is why they have invited her.'

'Who invited you?'

'What to do saab? Dying, but not talking about it.'

That was Ratan-babu.

The first thing I did as soon as morning dawned was to rush down to Guwahati without thinking anything. I was desperate to avoid Ratan-babu, that spirit which had taken possession of Shashwat and sent him back home. On the way I told myself that I would have to reach Guwahati to go anywhere else.

The same Guwahati which had seemed unrefined and alert two months earlier now seemed familiar, grave and warm. I first rushed off to see the Brahmaputra, as if he, too, was waiting for me. On my way to the river I realized what a relief it is sometimes to lose oneself in a crowd. As I approached the girls' hostel of Cotton College on one side of the Dighali Pukhuri, I saw a procession of girls carrying an idol of goddess Saraswati. The well-done-up, fragrant, ecstatic girls were blowing into conch shells and ringing bells. All at once I felt as if a handful of mustard seeds had swarmed across my scalp and rolled down my shirt.

I turned to look and found the girls giggling, hands on mouths. For a moment I wanted to believe that the Dighali Pukhuri was the most beautiful place in the Northeast.

I kept wandering about for a long time. I had decided that when I grew tired, I would check into a hotel and think in peace about where to go off to next. It was then that I ran into Mohanan Dada-aan on a street. He welcomed me with uncharacteristic warmth. He proposed that he would cook me dinner that night, and said I could stay in his room. He lived alone in Lachit Nagar. When we reached his house I saw a security guard sitting outside whom he asked to go home. He then said that fifteen days earlier there had been an 'accident' in the house because of which the guard had been hired.

By day three I wanted to run away from there but even after having run my finger over a map of the Northeast many times, I was unable to decide where I should go. This entry in my diary is from those three days:

> Situated upon a broad lane in this neighbourhood named after the Ahom warrior Lachit Borphukan is a small two-storeyed house at the front of which hangs a nameplate—M.R. Medhi, APS (Assam Police Service), 9th Lane, Lachit Nagar. In the broad courtyard are areca-nut, banana and coconut trees. There is a lawn in front and a backyard garden. Near the garage is a raised platform for the tulsi plant. A new diya is lit on the platform every evening. Behind the property is a flowing drain full of rotting garbage. Beyond the garbage is a school in which girls wearing red-bordered saris sing 'Raghupati Raghava Raja Ram' at prayer each morning. The prayer is sieved by the green curtains hanging from the windows before

it comes into the room where it is obscured by the smell of the dashang incense which is burned to keep the mosquitoes away.

The stairwell in the house is an art gallery. On the walls are landscapes painted by an amateur painter. Above it are oil paintings in large frames done by a steady hand. Animal heads carved out of wood and faces carved in bamboo roots adorn the stairs. Even a casual glance is sufficient to tell that this is the house of a cultured, art-loving family in which people talk and walk softly. The peace of the household is shattered many times in the day by the sobs and cries of children; the faces carved on the bamboo roots then seem ghoulish.

There are three children working as servants in the house. Two girls—one nine, the other seven—and a fourteen-year-old boy. Upon their prominent cheekbones and slitted eyes is embedded the fact that they are hill tribals. The mistress of the household and a man beat the girls very coldly. The intelligent-looking boy has his days, too, but his turn to be beaten comes around less often. The girls first whine in suppressed voices and then beg for mercy as if someone has yet again pressed a painful boil upon their skins. They try that their voices do not reach the ears of the tenants; this is something their mistress has strictly told them.

On sad evenings the lady's beautiful daughter memorizes the lines of an ancient English play in a loud voice in her room. She is a young actress in a local theatre troupe, a student of literature, and has brought home many trophies for having soulfully recited love poems. The screams and sobs of the servant girls emerging against the background of the young girl's dialogues transform this household into a theatre in which a realist play of the

Assamese middle class is staged each evening. At the same time, the evening prayers begin in the naamghar next door. Bhajans drenched in compassion float in the air.

A fortnight earlier, the police knocked on the door of the lower floor of this house in which a Manipuri family stays on rent. They interrogated a guest in the family for a little while and took him away. The guest had come from Imphal in search of work. The following morning the papers carried pictures of two corpses; one of which was that of the Manipuri guest. The other was that of a twenty-four-year-old Meitei boy who had been studying computer science in Guwahati University. Under the headline 'ULFA Joins Hands with the Manipuri Militant Organization, PREPAK' was the story that the man was the treasurer of PREPAK (People's Revolutionary Party of Kangleipak, Manipur) and had been working under directions from ULFA. The two dead men had been planning to blow up the office of the director general of police of Assam, it was said. A mobile phone, gelatin sticks, important documents and a map of Guwahati have been recovered from them, it was also reported.

The very next day the mistress of the house sent her son out of Assam to stay with a relative. She was afraid that either the police or the SULFA would bump him off because he knew that this was a fake encounter. The Manipuri family kept its doors shut for many days. No neighbour dared to go across and offer words of sympathy and condolence. The family finally went back to Manipur. The mother of the student killed in the fake encounter has filed a petition in an Imphal court.

That night, the mistress of the house as well as the Manipuri family had asked Mohanan-dada for help—he lived upstairs. He had called the police superintendent who had given his assurance that nothing untoward would happen. When Mohanan-dada saw the papers the following day he was shocked. He spoke to a senior official at Governor House and said that the police or the SULFA might kidnap him as well because they could think that he would write about the fake encounter even though he had no such intention. He knew nothing about Manipur or about PREPAK, he said. The officer advised him to hire a security guard and Mohanan-dada promptly obeyed.

When the papers publish news about encounters now, people of the neighbourhood glance meaningfully at each other but do not discuss that incident. In their hearts they criticize each other's insensitivity and feel the uncertain fear that anything at all can happen. The discussion, on the other hand, is about whether the Manipuri family left on its own or the landlady turned them out. The consensus is that they were asked to leave, because the comings and goings of the police and the SULFA were getting beyond the endurance of the landlady. Whenever Mohanan-dada is inebriated, he feels ashamed about his fear and his silence.

Life has become normal once more. A diya glows on the tulsi platform. The beatings of the servants have resumed. The girl keeps memorizing Shakespeare's dialogues. A 'to-let' signboard has been hung on the door downstairs.

~

The first truck that stopped on National Highway 37, which leads into the mountains, after I had stood for an hour and a half holding out a hand, astonished me. It was laden with fish and was bound from Andhra Pradesh to Jorhat. Jorhat became my destination.

Every house in Assam has a pond in its courtyard, every village has a small lake in its backyard. Just before Jorhat thirty-three small and big rivers join the Brahmaputra; in monsoon, the river spans 20 kilometres near Goalpara. It is possible that this he-river carries, alone, as much water as all the rivers of the country combined, yet fish is imported to Assam from other states. According to the fisheries department of Assam, the average yield from ponds in Haryana was on average 2,600 kilogrammes per hectare while the yield in Assam was 600 kilogrammes per hectare.

The driver, Bhyrappa, was a Kannadiga who, after a long period of unemployment, had taken a loan to buy this truck. He conducted an elaborate, unpleasant interview sitting behind a cloud of bidi smoke and, when dropping me off, advised in Hindi: 'Go back soon... The water here makes you impotent. Can't you see? Asomiya men can't catch the fish that is under their own legs.'

As one crosses Jorhat, it seems as if all greenery has suddenly dwarfed in size. Its average height under the thin, dappled shade of mimosa trees remains confined to three-and-a-half feet and it is hemmed in with barbed wire. There are thousands of people bobbing about in the sea of green which stretches far into the horizon. It is because of them that this lush greenery is possible but it is impossible to make out even one of their faces. These are the tea estates of Assam, whose owners—planters—live in Kolkata, Delhi, New York and London. The tea estates is one of those industries which bring the most foreign exchange into the country. This dwarfed greenery is always present as a background to the images of the Brahmaputra, the pretty girls dancing on Bihu and the rhinos of Kaziranga in those composite photographs created by travel agencies to present an image of 'Beautiful Assam'. The picture is real but the bright smiles on the faces of women who carry tall baskets on their backs are fake.

The workers being chewed up by the sea of green are from the Santhal, Oroan, Telanga and Munda tribes. Their ancestors were driven here by the British from Odisha, Bihar, Madhya Pradesh and Andhra Pradesh. They had been told by Bengali contractors—called 'coolie-catchers' then—that the tea plant rains money every time it is shaken. In three years, beginning May 1863, 84,915 people were first marched across central India and then herded onto steamers and brought to Jorhat. By June 1866, 30,000 of these workers had succumbed to dysentery, malaria, cholera and overwork. The will of the owners was law up until the dawn of the twentieth century. The lot of the workers was no better than that of slaves. Some of the tea estates of Assam still don't pay the mandatory minimum wage. Whips are made use of. These people are now half-slaves who have no contact at all with the rest of society. As ancient as the name 'Tea Tribe' is, still older is this song which offers a glimpse of these workers' lives:

> The babu says, 'Work!'
> The sardar says, 'I need more, catch me more.'
> The sahib says, 'I'll have your skin!'
> Oh Jaduram [a notorious coolie-catcher], why did you lie to us and bring us to Assam!

Some historians of Assam have labelled the tea labourers the 'Black Tribe' and people of Mongoloid stock the 'Yellow Tribe'. Approximately eleven lakh members of the 'Black

Tribe' had franchise in the state out of which seven lakh were permanent employees and four lakh daily wagers. There were fourteen MLAs from the 'Black Tribe' but the tea labourers cast the deciding vote in forty election seats. Through sardars and professional election managers, their votes have been plucked like tea leaves for the Congress Party over the last half century.

When I reached the estate, the bushes were being pruned, which rejuvenates the plant. Women, covered head to feet in plastic sheets, were sprinkling urea; men carrying cylinders on their backs were spraying insecticide. Their children were crawling about on their knees, picking leaves and trash. The mate and the manager were patrolling the estate.

~

Tinsukia feels like a small neighbourhood of Bihar. Hindi-speakers are aplenty. Trade is in the hands of Marwaris, the small retail in those of the Bengalis, labour and agriculture is done by the Hindi-speakers. Hindi-speakers were being massacred in the rest of Assam but here, in the strongholds of the Matak and Moran tribes—both of whom who support the ULFA—the streets rang with the lilt of Bhojpuri.

The fifth cybercafé of the town had opened up for business that day; its server was being upgraded in Dibrugarh. The internet would disconnect and, then, the wait... Middle-aged men would stagger out from curtained cabins, confused and disoriented because the porn videos they had been watching would have frozen and they were being charged from the time they took a seat to the time when they got up from it. The habits of the town's most modern, most net-savvy generation would be analyzed during the long wait.

Most boys use the internet to chat and most girls to surf matrimonial websites.

Using foul language in a chat can land one in jail.

If a boy is not to be seen for a fortnight, it can be concluded that he has had a serious fight with his girlfriend.

Marwari girls are fashionably dressed but call their boyfriends 'Bhaiya'. Their figures spoil soon because they eat desi ghee…

~

Only if a traveller is very lucky does he meets a man such as Rupah Chaliha. He was not merely a reporter for the *Purvanchal Prahari*. After his father, a freedom fighter, had died, he had washed cups and plates on a railway station, run a canteen, set up a cooperative society, bought an autorickshaw and plied it for two years. He had also run a bookshop which folded after two years, leaving him with a debt of 40,000 rupees. He was part of a mobile theatre as an actor which is where he met his wife Bani, herself an actor of renown from Sibsagar. He had toured villages performing magic tricks. He used to correspond with the famous magician of Rajasthan, Laxman Singh Gehlot, on the finer points of the art of performing magic—the old man must have believed Chaliha to be a contemporary in age. After the death of the magician, his son Ashok Gehlot (the former chief minister of Rajasthan) wrote to Chaliha asking that he keep in touch with the Gehlot family and love them as a father would. Within two hours of meeting he became Rupah-da to me. He found me a room on very little rent, one among many which had been lying vacant for months on the roof of a sprawling hotel. His scooter, which would sputter to life only after being kick-started ten or twelve times, was always available for me. Latika Katt, too, had ridden this scooter when she was in Jorhat to look for her husband, Balbir Singh Katt, who was once the dean of the sculpture department of BHU. Katt, one of the more prominent sculptors of the country, vanished from Benaras one day and has never been found.

The hotel was a maze. Towering over the roof was a vast pipal tree, all the leaves of which had fallen. The moon seemed stuck among its branches. Two cadres of ULFA had been 'encountered' in the hotel few days earlier; since then, the rooms had remained largely unoccupied and unlocked. I could sleep in any of the rooms in turn and dream different dreams. The establishment was patronized by the occasional businessman whose every secret would be laid bare at the counter the morning after. There was a Bhojpuri woman who would tell the manager in an unfussy tone, as if she were reporting a leaky tap or a fused bulb: 'Number 325 is useless. He uses his tongue like a bullock.'

Some five hundred steps from the hotel, on Rangora Road, lived Sanjay Khaitan, the hero of Tinsukia, and spokesman for the terrible, oppressive boredom of small towns. He was learning the ropes of the family business. His father owned a bungalow, a tea garden and many businesses. In between monitoring the gossip of his staff and idly turning the pages of the ledgers, he would often find time to invite me home for meals. He owned a big, long car, in which he used to roam the streets of Tinsukia, and when he was done roaming, he would go to either the district magistrate or the police superintendent and shake their hands. The toughest part of the exercise for me would be to answer the two questions which he would ask suddenly, and apropos nothing at all.

'What did you think the first time you saw me?'
'How do you find me?'

~

A tea garden comprises two worlds. One can sense time from the era of the British planters stagnating in the silence of the vast bungalows of the estate managers. The hats hanging underneath red-tiled ceilings, rifles, tiger-skins, bone-china tea-sets, stale editions of foreign newspapers, billiards matches in decrepit planters' clubs, tables reserved for decades and ranks of servants standing with their arms folded, eager to serve on weary evenings, all lead into an ancient world which now exists elsewhere only in photographs. Cars have taken the place of horses and after every drink the latest share prices of the tea companies on the stockmarket come marching into conversations.

The villages in which the Tea Tribes live are called 'lines'. Patients suffering from tuberculosis live in abject poverty and wait for death here. Incidents of snakebite are narrated with the same ease with which one describes slumber interrupted by mosquito bites.

One night I met both the worlds in one place.

A rickshaw-wala took me to the green gloom of the Panitola estate in pouring rain. The new theatre group in town, 'Ankur', was staging an anti-communalism play. Bespectacled Bengali and Assamese women, their hair adorned with jasmine, sat bundled up in costly shawls in the front row, bathed in the light from bulbs which flickered in rhythm with the thud-thud of generators. They were like Chekhov's heroines: devotees of art. A group of wild-haired young men sheltering underneath polythene sheets and tattered umbrellas ran riot on one side of the seating area. In between, seated upon sacks on the ground were faces with yellow eyes which were dozing unconcerned. The stage was well decorated. Taking cues from cinema, a projector was used to introduce the names of the actors to the audience. Most of them were clerks and cashiers from the tea garden. There was a showy invocation during which two tribal girls stood on one foot for seven minutes in front of Lord Krishna printed on a calendar, trying to control their giggles. When a Muslim character—a victim of communal violence—walked on to the stage bemoaning his fate, the wild-haired boys shouted: 'There's the new engineer. That fucker is a butcher.'

It was difficult to hear anything over the catcalls and the whistles but the ladies of the front row did not waver their attention one bit. This was a night of festivity for them and, over its course, they would have to closely scrutinize each other's attire and aesthetics. They also had to discharge the grave responsibility of giving away the awards to the actors.

~

Before proceeding to the Barbetta Line, Pravin Dutt, leader of the Workers' Union affiliated to the Asom Gana Parishad, put on his suit and sprayed perfume upon himself. While he was doing this, his mother gave me a cream-roll-like snack made out of rice flour which had been offered as prasad. As soon as he finished wiping his battered Premier Padmini clean, another leader, Ashok Das, arrived. Soon after we left it started to pour and the car broke down. We pushed the car a fair distance, hoping to jumpstart it, but couldn't.

The two of them would address every married woman in the Line as 'bhauji'—sister-in-law. Both would light a fresh cigarette before entering a new house—perhaps this was a trademark of combative trade union leaders. They would criticize the leaders of the Assam Chah Mazdoor Sangha (ACMS), which was affiliated to the Congress, and say, 'Don't you worry. Our Union will set everything right.' The ACMS was equally popular among owners and workers. Most of the organization's labour leaders are now owners of tea estates. The president of the ACMS, Paban Singh Ghatowar, was born in Dumardalang Line; he now owns one hundred-bigha tea estate in the town of Moran. An MLA for fifteen years, Rameswar Dhanowar owns a two hundred-bigha tea estate in Pengri; the secretary of the Tingrai Circle, Rajendra Prasad Singh, has a three hundred-bigha estate in Bordubi; and former labour minister Dileshwar Tanti, has a hundred-bigha estate in Dum Duma. After every election, it is said, at least one labour leader becomes the proud owner of a tea estate.

Old labourers from the tea estates say, 'We use the hand to pluck leaves, we use the hand to eat, if we ditch the election symbol of the hand, ghosts will catch us.' So... It was the fear of spirits which had been spurring these people on since Independence to cast their votes for the Congress Party.

A young woman wearing an unbuttoned blouse was

filling water at a hand pump. Her breasts were so shrivelled that she was unconcerned about whether they would be seen. Many TB patients were sitting underneath arecanut trees outside the Line, staring dully. Each quarter had been given to two families, and was bare except for a dirt floor, soot-blackened walls, a few aluminium utensils and some clothes. A few rare households had sewing-machines, pressure cookers and calendars with an image of Jesus Christ and these words: 'All ye sufferers! Come unto me, I shall give thee heaven!' There were many small children with distended bellies and a few teenaged skeletal boys in the Line. They followed us in a small procession, careful to maintain distance.

A bhauji assumed that we had come to drink handiya. Covering the three heavy glasses she was carrying with the end of her sari, Bhauji requested Pravin to tell the mahajan to not come to her house. She had borrowed 200 rupees from him five years earlier; she had paid him 1,200 rupees in interest and given the man innmumerable glasses of handiya yet the debt hadn't been paid.

Pravin cracked a joke, 'Bhauji is elder to her husband by a year on paper.'

'That soot-face! He makes fake papers to send women retire.' She was angry because she was ten years younger than her husband.

Illiteracy is taken advantage of to record fudged ages. Labourers are retired early and re-employed on a daily-wage basis. Children, too, are stated as being older than they actually are and put to work. Fifteen fortunate children of that Line were child labourers; others were considered unworthy even of that. Labourers working on a permanent basis were paid 37 rupees and 60 paise for a minimum of 21 kilogrammes of tea plucked—the minimum wage guarantee in those days was 49 rupees per day. Four kilogrammes of tea leaves is processed into 1 kilogramme of black tea, which retails at 80 rupees per kilogramme. Bhauji led us to a crèche where a lone swing made out of a car tyre was supervising the children. The dispensary—from where the compounder, when he arrived, would dispense a red-coloured medicine for every ailment—was shut.

School was in session. Fifty-eight students out of a total strength of seventy-eight were in attendance and were being taught by two teachers, also on a daily-wage basis. Only the children of the labourers employed on a permanent basis can be admitted to the school, which explained the procession of children trailing us. As soon as we entered the classroom the children raised their hands to their ears in salutation and chimed: 'Namaste sir!'

I enjoyed talking to those frail, malnourished children, clad only in underwear and wiping their runny noses. They spoke in Sadri, the language of the plantations, which is a mix of their original tribal tongue, Assamese, the language uses in that particular district, and Hindi. We met Bhauji outside the classroom, standing with the glasses still in her hand. She said, 'It is good that the Union boys come now and then. Moneylenders and handiyawalas are our only visitors.'

Finding that the woman was still following us exhausted Ashok Das's patience. He said to Pravin: 'That Kamaljit, the only matric-pass boy of this Line, is secretary of ACMS. Bringing these useless people into the party is the same as pressing sand for oil.'

The children looked out of the window in the classroom and chanted. 'Goodbye. Namaste sir!'

It has not been possible, even after these many years, for the rest of Assamese society to build any relationship with these tea-estate labourers who live within their barbed-wire enclosures. Isolation is their biggest enemy. The Assamese people appreciate their submissiveness because they, unlike the Muslims from Mymensingh, have never tried to settle on their land.

I had another opportunity to visit the Panitola Tea Estate, which is part of the Hindustan Lever group, with another tea leader, Israel Nanda. A Sardarji, looking for an opportunity to speak English amidst the lush greenery, was manager there. He told us that an estate manager does not work ten to five like other officers do. He is a friend to the labourers. Involved 24x7 in their lives. The Tea Tribes love the gardens, he said. And, because of their tribal origins, they see god in the tea bushes.

Drops of birdshit gleamed upon the smooth leaves of tea in the bright sun.

~

After spending a few nights in a tea estate I began to glimpse the parallel government which was levying a 'war-fund' tax of an average of 2 rupees on the production of each kilogramme of tea. The cadre of the ULFA based in Tinsukia and Dibrugarh would meet the managers and owners of tea estates, politely ask them for their licensed weapons and take them away. Not a peep of protest would escape the managers and owners. Their vehicles were being used by the cadres for their operations. The supporters of the ULFA were pleased that their boys were largely successful in preventing money from leaving Assam and were teaching corrupt traders and officials a lesson.

The owner of every tea estate, big or small, was paying up without protest but, from this regular payment, it was possible only to gauge the quantum of profit in the trade and not the actual might of the tea lobby. It was this lobby which toppled the Prafulla Kumar Mahanta government in 1991 when extortion crossed all limits and created the conditions for 'Operation Bajrang' against the ULFA. To bring together the scattered strands of this story was to feel the heat of the nexus of capital and politics wreathed in the vapour rising up from a cup of hot tea.

It is said that in 1990, when the ULFA was at its peak strength, it was considered to be an extension of government itself. Not a leaf could quiver in any village in Assam without the express wish of the ULFA. That year the ULFA wrote a letter to all the major tea-producing companies; Tata Tea, McLeod Russel, Unilever and Macneill Magor, and summoned them to Dibrugarh to discuss ways to ensure the economic development of Assam. These officials reached Dibrugarh on 29 June after having secured written undertakings from their respective employers that the establishment would take care of their families in the event of any mishap during the meeting.

There, their chauffeurs were dismissed, the officers were ordered to take the wheels of their respective cars and to follow a boy riding a scooter. The boy piloted the officials through the evening gloom to a tea garden where the driveway from the main gate to the manager's bungalow was lined with ULFA cadres, all bearing arms. Tapan Datta, the chief of the ULFA Dibrugarh unit, and the man who would initiate the discussion on development, was sitting inside the manager's bungalow. Two vice-presidents serving with McLeod Russel, Ravi Rikhe and Gautam Barua, were first taken inside. Tapan Datta asked them, 'You have been looting Assam for ages. Aren't you people ashamed of yourselves?'

When Ravi Rikhe tried to explain the schemes his company had implemented to boost local development, Tapan Datta became angry. 'Stop your lecturing! We want one crore from your company next month.' In three-and-a-half hours he fixed the amount of money that was to be extorted from the executives of the most wealthy tea estates of Assam.

The apex body of the tea industry, the Tea Planters' Association, had met the chief minister, Prafulla Kumar Mahanta, for help before sending their executives to the meeting with the ULFA. The chief minister had told them that they must help themselves. Escorting the managers back from the tea estate, Tapan Datta warned them that if they went to the chief minister again, their local managers would be killed and the tea gardens left to run wild.

Most companies paid up before the deadline.

Unilever, the multinational, owns seven gardens in Dum Duma, and Brooke Bond and Lipton are its two big companies which buy up to 60 per cent of the tea auctioned in Guwahati annually. This group was ordered to pay three-and-a-half crore in all to the War Fund. This was a dead loss. The company decided to shut down operations in Assam instead of paying the ULFA. But this was their ultimate option; they were to first knock on the doors of the Centre. The Indian arm of Unilever, Hindustan Lever, sent an SOS to its London office. The head office got in touch with Kuldip Nayar, then the Indian high commissioner, who advised the government to take stern action against the ULFA and prevent the situation in Assam from spiralling out of control.

After a brief hesitation the Centre agreed to suspend the government headed by Prafulla Kumar Mahanta because it had proved to be ineffectual. Research and Analysis Wing (RAW), Intelligence Bureau (IB) and the intelligence agencies of the Indian Army prepared a joint plan to quickly evacuate the employees of Unilever from the seven tea gardens. A control room was set up in Delhi to ensure coordination between London, Kolkata and Dum Duma. The initial plan was to bring the employees to Guwahati and Kolkata in an Indian Airlines plane. This was later changed and it was decided that on 8 November, the date of the secret operation, a Boeing 737 would be sent to an old airstrip near Dum Duma. The executives were woken at midnight on 7 November, told to prepare themselves and their families for flight, and reach the airstrip within two hours. From there they were flown safely to Kolkata.

Lieutenant General Ajai Singh had been transferred to the eastern zone, Tezpur, from the western command on the Indo-Pak border in the month of September. He was to be the Corps Commander of the front. The chief of Army staff, Sunith Francis Rodrigues, had tasked him with keeping an eye on the law and order situation in Assam. On 18 November, the Commanding Officer of all the Army units serving in the east, J.S. Brar, called Ajai

Singh to Kolkata and informed him that the Army was to be deployed in Assam. He was also told that the security agencies in the state were defunct and Singh would have to build his own secret network. It was also vital, Brar said, that the local police be kept completely out of the loop because a large section of the force was in cahoots with the ULFA.

On 26 November, thirty thousand soldiers from across India were pulled in and stationed in ULFA strongholds. That midnight, President R. Venkataraman signed an order suspending the Asom Gana Parishad government; the ULFA had already been declared a terrorist organization. The state government became void on 28 November. When Assam awoke the following morning, olive green uniforms had fanned out across villages, houses were being searched and ULFA sympathizers were being arrested and taken away to secret locations. Operation Bajrang had begun. On 4 December a mass grave was discovered in Lakhipathar, near Tinsukia, with fifteen bodies rotting in it. Many among the dead were officers and executives working in the tea gardens who had been kidnapped. The date of operation had leaked in spite of all the secrecy and the precautions. All the prominent leaders of ULFA, along with chief Paresh Baruah, had slipped into Bangladesh.

~

The affection which Rupah-da felt for me was rapidly transforming into a big-brotherly sense of possessiveness—a dangerous sign. Another friend, Husain-da, was a trader whose ancestors had migrated from Ghazipur district in Uttar Pradesh had and settled in Tinsukia. He organized a banquet in my honour one night in which he sang Bhojpuri songs, accompanying himself on the congo, and we had an enjoyable gathering of friends. Filled with a sense of utter responsibility, Rupah-da would constantly lecture me about my drinking. But that night, too, I drank my fill and sang to my heart's content; despite him forbidding me to do so. He became so vexed with my drinking that he stopped his scooter on a deserted street at midnight and left me there. In the morning he counselled me further and said, 'If you want to see the jungles of Arunachal, go immediately to Mohanbari and secure an Inner-Line Permit.'

Standing behind me in the queue in front of the office of the Deputy Commissioner of Arunachal Pradesh in Mohanbari was Meghnath Borpujari who was swearing at every coquetry of the Bengali woman sitting behind the counter enclosed by wire netting. I felt that the Assamese language doesn't have many cusswords which was why he was having to fashion metaphors. He was standing in line to have permits issued for the entire family of one of the officials of his department. He had made a mistake with one of the forms in the morning; this was his second round of being pushed around. I called him over, gave him my place and stood behind him; he became embarrassed and fell silent for a long time. The clerk had overlapping teeth like Moushmi Chatterjee, which gave her a pretty smile, but she would do so only when someone would say 'thank you' to her. A flick of her head would leave a single lock of hair trembling upon her cheek. Once the permit was issued I stopped Meghnath and pointed out the trembling lock to him; he became very happy. We went up together to the counter and excessively thanked her to gaze at that shivering lock of hair.

Meghnath started with me perched on the carrier of his bicycle to drop me off at the bus stop but we changed our minds midway; he took me to a country-liquor store instead. In the falling twilight he downed two glasses of tepid homebrew and became sad that so poor had his vision become that he could no longer observe such a wonderful sight as a woman's swaying hair. He was very depressed, and on the verge of tears, so he asked me to drop him home on the bicycle. The moon was out by the time we reached Lahul, his village. He said to his mother, 'Imagine! This boy came from Delhi and has given me complete rights over himself. What a big thing that is!'

His mother cooked all possible manner of Assamese delicacies in great haste and served them along with fish curry and rice. When she and Meghnath's sisters began to ask after my welfare, I remembered the faces of my father's sisters, my mother's sisters and brothers whom I hadn't met in decades and whom I was unlikely to ever meet again. In the morning, after having industriously polished off a bottle of homebrew, sharing it equally with me, he spread a mat on a handcart and installed me upon it. Pulling the handcart himself, he took me to buy paan. He would stop at each house in the village and announce: 'Come quick villagers, and look. Feast your eyes upon my guest. He has given me complete right upon himself.'

The procession kept swelling in size. I was forbidden from stepping off the handcart because I was their guest. I would be asked the philosophical question over and over at every door: Why was I wandering about, having left behind my home and family? I had no answer. The following morning a number of women and children came to see me off at the bus stop. I left with a heavy heart.

When I opened my fist to pay the bus conductor I found the two-rupees and a five-rupees notes, all crumpled up and grubby, which those women had taken from the tied-up corner of their saris and given me. 'To find love!' is what I should have replied to their question. But, by then, the time had passed and so had that village.

~

Rupah-da handed me over to Nature's Beckon in front of the Tinsukia Railway Station. When the Tata 407 mini-bus finally left—after having seated flustered passengers arriving from god knows where—fowl stuffed into a wicker-basket kept underneath a seat cackled. Potatoes were popping out from a hole in a sack and rolling about on the floor. We were eighteen passengers in all, including a ten-year-old, travelling with a group of experts who worked for Nature's Beckon, an NGO that promoted environmental awareness. Our destination was the jungles of Namdapha in Changlang in Arunachal Pradesh—Namdapha is the highest peak of the region. These jungles, which abut the border with Burma, rise up from swampy wetlands in the plains to snow-covered mountains and spread over an area of 2,000 square kilometres. There is such geographic diversity here that multiple seasons co-exist over contiguous territory. From the jhapi hats, binoculars, packets of crisps and the keen desire to hear the opinions of strangers on the varieties of forests found in different geographical regions of the world, it was clear everyone had done their homework well.

Soumyadeep, the young director of NB, had tried to lighten the atmosphere at opportune times with jokes and tales of travels in the wild but he spoke in the toneless manner of a tour guide in a rush. No tales were told to him in reply. Soon, a freshly minted journalist, Pem Thi Gohain, launched an interrogation about the salary structure at the paper I worked for, and about the editor who was brilliant enough to send me on this journey in the Northeast. I distanced myself from him by speaking in English and, pretending to be absorbed in the landscape, shrank into myself and looked out of the window. It wasn't possible to tell any more lies.

A tyre punctured in Digboi. The driver propped the vehicle on a makeshift jack built out of a pile of bricks and stood on the side of the road, thumbing down trucks to borrow a tyre-iron from. This would take a while and I left for a short walkabout in town.

In Digboi are oil-wells; neighbourhoods do not have names but are identified by golai numbers. There are also small hills dotted with red bungalows from the British era. Each bungalow, once occupied by a single British family, is now shared by many households. Digboi is a peaceful, hilly town where, if one has eaten a heavy breakfast of rice, one would be sleepy and bored.

We left and, soon after, the driver stopped the vehicle in Margherita. While the rest of us ate, he went off to have the puncture repaired. Santwana Bharali, aka Poppy, was our tour coordinator. She had an MSc in Botany; her cheeks would dimple when she smiled. A co-passenger was a psychology nut. He said quietly, 'She has gone to the puncture-shop because she wants to see that tube swell up.' I concurred. But when she opened her purse and paid the mechanic, I silently condemned the influence of Freud upon the manner in which I had agreed with him. Archana Niyog, like a homely girl, was inviting everyone to eat.

The large yellow signboard which marks the beginning of the Stilwell Road flashed past us near the railway crossing in the town of Ledo. The road, built during the Second World War at enormous cost in terms of the lives of soldiers and labourers, originates in Jairampur in Arunachal Pradesh, enters Burma, spans Kachin territory and terminates in Kunming in China. One of the longstanding demands in the region is the reopening of the Stilwell Road so that trade may flourish, but our relations with China are rocky.

Ledo is a vast colliery. Dust enveloped gigantic heaps of coal in a black mist. Open-cast mining had given the town the colour of fear.

The olive-green of battle fatigues became more and more concentrated once we entered Arunachal Pradesh. A state of high alertness has become permanent here after 1962 when China defeated India in war. We were stopped at every checkpoint to be interrogated and for our permits to be examined; it was night by the time we were done. Before this, when evening fell, everyone had looked out at the twilight, suddenly silent—perhaps they were looking at the innermost colours of their mind which were imprinted upon the sky. Then, everyone dozed. Within the forest glowed pinpoints of fire like diyas which were, in reality, tree-felling techniques. Instead of the telltale thwack-thwack of axe on tree trunk, a small hole is drilled and a fire set within it. The embers smoulder for many days before the tree finally comes crashing down. In many places forests were being burned down to make way for jhum cultivation. Those fires were much bigger. Only 2 per cent of the total territory of Arunachal is under permanent cultivation; either as terraced fields or as flatland plots.

The bus crossed one of the gates of Namdapha. In the lights of the headlamps, a shaggy animal was galloping along. Eyes opened, shoulders joined and heads came together. Poppy quacked in a sleepy voice, 'Porcupine! Porcupine! I know very well that was a porcupine.'

The animal vanished under the bushes on the side of the road. The ten-year-old had found his long-awaited opportunity to lay hands upon his father's binoculars—so what if it was dark? The mini-bus stopped near a waterfall where a foul smell was in the air. There was a herd of swamp deer nearby which is recognizable by its rank odour. Just as the bandit Ratnakar transformed into the poet Valmiki, who wrote the *Ramayana*, Jain-ul-Abedeen aka Benu Daku, a veteran hunter from Tinsukia, had incarnated into an environmentalist. He said, snorting, 'This is a very foolish animal. They are spooked by torches and can't run. Hunters get them easy.'

It was a 4-kilometre hike from the waterfall to the resthouse. All of us shouldered our bags. We trooped into the darkness in a long queue, our path lighted by torches. Buzzing crickets were shaking up the entire forest. On our left was a deep gorge at the bottom of which the Noa Dihing River roared. The silence of the forest could be heard in the pauses between the crump-crump of footsteps. In those moments it felt as if the act of measuring time is a joke which man plays to keep himself in a state of delusion. Elephant dung, a deer's hoofprints, tyre marks all became mysteries to be deciphered at leisure. All at once, Benu shone his light into the gorge as if looking for something. He stopped, then said sotto voce, 'There might be a tigress nearby.'

A commotion followed, which crumpled up our single file and transformed it into a huddle. The effect of torchlight on tigers was discussed in whispers, with books being quoted from along with mentions of their publishers and prices. This was a serious moment but something seemed out of joint. I don't know why, but I thought, This is a new profession for Benu. He and Soumyadeep are injecting a dose of excitement into these middle-class nature-lovers so that their trip becomes memorable.

As soon as we reached the resthouse, all of us sweat-soaked travellers called out to our gods and collapsed, using our backpacks as cushions upon which to straighten our strained backs. Water to boil rice bubbled upon makeshift stoves made out of bricks, a safe corner for the women to sleep in was scouted. A whistle went off shrilly and at length; everyone gathered round and the experts answered questions on Namdapha in the light of a kerosene lantern.

The tiger, and three species of leopard—the common leopard, the clouded leopard and the rare snow leopard—inhabit Namdapha. The red panda is also to be found here. The Namdapha Tiger Reserve was set up because this area is the perfect habitat for felines: it has flowing water, shade and abundant prey. The last three make up the ideal environmental cycle. Some creatures such as the flying squirrel, the white hornbill and the howler monkey make the reserve their home because of geographical features which are unique to the area. Chakma refugees from Bangladesh have been rehabilitated in a village called Gandhi Gram situated inside the forest. They hunt and eat elephants. Hunting has decimated the elephant population. Lisu refugees from Burma live in the jungle, too. They are skilled at hunting tigers. Tiger-bone liquor is much in demand in China. Tiger whiskers are used to manufacture sex toys. The wide expanse of the jungle is manned by just thirteen employees who can't even manage to shut all the gates of the reserve. There is no electricity and the water from the Noa Dihing River is used for drinking...

After these stark truths were underlined in many different ways, the dancing flames reflected on the walls took on a new meaning. The deep silence of the forest spread inside the minds of us exhausted travellers. The whistle went off again, shrill and long; rice and bean curry was distributed. Later, all of us washed dishes in candlelight. In a little while snores could be heard.

It was raining in the morning. Binoculars and cameras jumped out of their carrying cases and kept waiting for a long time. In a steady drizzle, we were ferried across the Noa Dihing in two batches. Vimal Gogoi and Mridul Phukan were identifying birds and animals from their calls. The deep silence of the forest suddenly made itself felt once more, and I thought, In a crowd, we utterly lose the ability to feel because we are trying to frantically communicate something or the other and this takes up all our attention. Thus, walking underneath the dripping forest canopy on the thick carpet of fallen leaves and sodden mulch, I felt a sense of regret. This forest had everything I wanted, but what I missed was the connection that I feel with a solitary tree by a roadside because there is no one between me and the tree.

Poppy showed us a twig on which grew a layer of what seemed like white mould. She said, 'Look, this lichen is proof, there is no pollution here.' She picked up a berry from the ground and said, 'The pahu eats the flesh of this fruit and the porcupine its seed. They they help propagate these seeds all over the forest.'

'This pahu, is it a bird?' She laughed. I understood that I had made yet another mistake in wringing meaning from the Assamese language.

'Pahu is not a bird. In Hindi, pahu is called hiran,' Archana taught me.

We had climbed from a height of forty metres to two hundred and fifty metres over rocky, uneven terrain. Thin red leeches swarmed up our shoes. They soon began to crawl into our socks and everyone started to look for salt—the best antidote for leeches—which we had all forgotten to bring. Tikendrajit, from Barpeta, had long been scratching his head. A leech had fastened itself to his scalp and was turgid with blood. I pulled it off.

A tribal boy, Lat Gam Singpho, was accompanying our party as guide. He used his dao to cut strips of green cane and made himself a crown. When everyone crowded around him demanding a crown, he made one for each. A lengthy photo session ensued. As soon as they wore the crowns a chemical imbalance ensued in their brains and, with the sounds of 'He hai hua, chi chai chung!', mischief began. In that green cane they had found an excuse to express their natural reactions to their perception of the ignorant and backward ways of the tribals. Except for the girls, everyone tried the keen-edged Singpho machete on the trees.

After noon, the sun came out and the forest filled with colour. We heard the cracking of bamboo somewhere. A small herd of elephants was passing through which all of us saw only in our imaginations. A sudden shower drenched us in the evening and so we didn't need the services of a boat to cross the Noa Dihing on our way back. Many other environmentalists came to us at night and—eating chicken curry and rice—gave us much useful information on crocodiles, hornbills and elephants. That night, people narrated their experiences of the jungle. Someone was terrified by the sight of an elephant brought up close by his binoculars, another slyly transformed anecdote into personal experience. Archana told us the heartrending story of the death of a calving cow and her attachment to the orphaned calf. Soumyadeep often dreamt of wild elephants surrounding him and of a forest-goddess who would come to his rescue. Lat Gam Singpho, who now lived in the forest, had once been a ward-boy in a hospital. His story was exceptional.

'... I can face down a tiger with a dao in hand but corpses scare me to death. The doctors in the hospital conspired so that I would lose my job. They put a new shirt on a corpse and propped it against a wall. A burning cigarette was put between its fingers, loose change was in its pocket and a dao was slung from a belt at its waist. The corpse was pointed out to me and I was sent to summon it. When it didn't hear my calls I put a hand on its shoulder and then took off running. That day, for the first time in my life, I drank a boiling cup of tea in one breath.'

This was the first genuine story of a tribal wandering about in a jungle of dead souls.

Amid the marathon of snoring, the ten-year-old snuggled up to me and demanded a story. He was unhappy and couldn't sleep. I scoured all the corners of my memory but found no tale suitable for a young child. All my stories were tagged with an 'A' certificate. I first felt a surge of self-pity, then came a glimmer of self-realization: As a child, I would doubt every story I heard. And as my pessimism towards them grew, they slipped out of my memory. He said, 'Let's go for a stroll outside, maybe you will remember a story there.'

Outside the resthouse, a furry creature floated across the milky-white beam cast by the flashlight. Another followed it. It was a pair of flying squirrels playing catch, which the team of experts tramping about all day hadn't been able to spot. A thin membrane connects the fore and hind legs of the rodent on both sides. Using tree branches as a runway, it gathers speed and launches itself. The membrane fills up with air and the squirrel glides from tree to tree.

My work had been made easy. All I needed to do was to tie a forest-god's cloak around the boy's neck, sling a Singpho dao around his waist, and place him on the back of a flying squirrel. Now he could himself tell the stories of the secrets of the jungles.

~

The first batch of one thousand plastic replicas of hornbill beaks had recently arrived from Delhi which had been distributed in the villages of the Nyishi tribe around Namdapha. Lat Gam Singpho had a question for Bharat Sundaram, project officer with the Asian Elephant Research and Conservation Centre, Bangalore: 'Will elephants made out of plastic be distributed among the Chakma refugees living in the west of Namdapha?' The Chakmas eat elephant, which they hunt with poisoned arrows. It takes them half an hour to bring down an animal but the preparation for the hunt lasts for many days.

Young Bharat Sundaram was then on a trek in the Northeast, accompanied by porters laden with provisions and tents. He was tracking footprints and sampling elephant dung to determine their numbers. A nationwide elephant census was underway. The Northeast was a special zone where the very existence of elephants was under threat in many areas; many of their old stomping grounds and corridors of passage had been wiped out. However, it was the hornbill Bharat was really interested in. This was because of those traits in the bird which are only expected of humans. Bharat had photographed a rufous-headed Hornbill in Namdapha. This species of hornbill had never before been spotted in India and it was being treated as a new find.

The hornbill is a colourful, beautiful bird with an extraordinarily large beak. When the female lays eggs, she takes a maternity leave of four months. She emerges from the nest only when the young are able to fly. During this time the male guards the nest. He brings food for his wife and children. Some species of hornbills form cooperative societies. Many pairs get together to hatch eggs and to look after the brooding mothers. Pairs mate for life and remain faithful to each other. The beauty of the hornbill is also its curse. The Nagas use their feathers to adorn their headdresses. Many tribes of Arunachal Pradesh, including the Nyishi, use hornbill beaks as ornaments on their crowns. They wait for the male to return to the nest with food for its brooding mate and kill it. The flesh and the fat of the hornbill are considered aphrodisiac. Itinerant quacks who examine people on roadsides in full view of curious gawkers keep hornbill beaks with which they lure the loveless and the superstitious. This bird is rapidly dwindling in numbers; it is rarely spotted even in dense forests.

It was the officials of the forestry department and the Wildlife Trust of India who, after a great deal of thought, jointly came up with the idea of the replicas. The beaks distributed in the Nyishi villages had been manufactured in Delhi on order. Each had cost 15 rupees to make. Since one can't charge money from the hornbills for saving their lives, they were being distributed gratis to the tribals. The officers and the NGOs hoped that the tribals would reconcile these plastic toys with their religious beliefs and the hunting of the hornbill for use in headdresses would stop. Some organizations felt that plastic is harmful to the environment and the tribals should be given wooden beaks. Even better, they should be trained to carve beaks so that they could find employment.

Some people in the villages had kept the plastic beaks, but the ones with the original article were making fun of them. Now the danger was that the remaining hornbills in the forest would also be wiped out due to this conflict between the villagers. This was why Lat Gam Singpho wanted to put his question to Bharat Sundaram.

Bharat had also visited Gandhi Gram, the furthest village on India's frontier, in the far south end of Namdapha. Lisu refugees from Burma have been settled there. Anyone who visits with kerosene and sugar is welcomed in the village as an honoured guest. The nearest weekly market is a three-day walk each way. They barter goods with fish which is hunted with the aid of a local anaesthetic. The Lisu examine the moss growing on rocks standing in the river and gauge the size of the fish from the marks made on the moss by the fishes' mouth. They then take the leaves of a particular tree which has narcotic properties, grind them and stir the paste into the water. The drugged fish float belly-up on the surface. The fish were not for sale but, yes, they could be bartered for kerosene.

~

In the year Kuru Hasang was born in the Ziro valley, the Apatani tribe was yet to come across that invention known as the wheel. This, even though the Apatani are considered to be the most modern among the tribes of Arunachal for having innovated the concepts of fixed cultivation and irrigation. Even today, jhum cultivation is carried out over more than 90 per cent of the land by setting fire to forests. In 1963, when Hasang was admitted to the Army School in Bhubaneshwar, his father ritually sacrificed an egg on the village border before letting him go out into the limitless, unknown world. Within five years of leaving his village, Hasang was commissioned into the Air Force and became a fighter pilot and flew MIGs. In 1978, he came back to his village in Arunachal, after it had attained statehood, to try his hand at politics after having retired as Flight Lieutenant. At that time, the middle-aged Kuru Hasang, after having lost multiple elections, was the chief secretary of the Arunachal Pradesh Congress Committee.

His wife ran a medical store in the Hapoli neighbourhood of Ziro.

Many tribes of Arunachal Pradesh, including the Nocte, the Khampti, the Singpho, the Nyishi and the Tagin, have their own heroes—exceptions to the norm—who, owing to coincidences, have managed to experience many lives in the one life they lived. They have vaulted distances which has taken the rest of humanity many thousands of years to trudge over. The recorded ancient history of this area, too, is merely three hundred years old. More than sixty tribes live in Arunachal and there are more than fifty known languages. Every retired governmental officer who has served in the area has many a story in which they tell of how, in the initial days of their posting, accustomed as they were to viewing nudity as scandalous, they would not even look at the tribals. What happened when they did start looking is another story altogether…

The state of Arunachal has itself similarly launched headlong into democracy. Before Independence, the official name of the region was, simply, 'Tribal Area'. A few British surveyors would travel there accompanied by armed battalions, scouting for opportunities to build roads and lay down railway lines, to extend avenues of trade for the East India Company further into countries in the east. In 1954, the Kameng, Siang, Subansiri, Lohit, Tirap and Tuensang divisions were combined into the North East Frontier Agency (NEFA) which was administered by the Foreign Ministry for a long time. After 1972, Tuensang went to Nagaland and the rest of the divisions coalesced into Arunachal Pradesh. Post 1962, after the war with China, the Central government invested blindly in roads and communication networks here, and the investment shows. A population of merely nine lakh lives in an area of 78,000 square kilometres but telephone poles stand tall in every forest. The Army regularly flies sorties from bases in Siliguri and Dibrugarh, ferrying rations, political leaders, officers and soldiers—an exercise that costs an average of 4 crore rupees per day. There are close to one hundred helipads in the state. In all of India, the maximum number of mishaps—mainly due to helicopters losing their way in fog and crashing—in which ministers, chief ministers and pilots have lost their lives have occurred in Arunachal Pradesh.

I wanted to visit Hapoli and meet Kuru Hasang and his wife. The idea was to conduct a long interview on his memories of the time when he came back to Ziro on his first furlough from the Air Force. But I got distracted and reached Tawang instead.

That day in Bhalukpong, the remnants of a poet lying dormant within the soul of a Buddhist monk of the Mahayana order decided to come awake. He only said, 'Tawang has played for two hours in the light of the new sun by the time dawn breaks over the rest of the world.' I had the names of lamas given to me by friends in Benares, lamas who had studied theology in Sarnath and who now lived in monasteries in Arunachal Pradesh. So I set out on a very long, serpentine road which was shrouded in fog and covered in a desert of snow. It has never again been possible to see more shades of blue in the sky.

Before I reached Bomdila, I had never imagined that, in the first and second gears, a Tata Sumo understands its driver's feelings like a faithful horse understands its rider's. It takes a special set of ears to become a driver on these harsh mountains; ears which can discern the whispers, wails and sobs of an engine underneath its roar. And a special kind of sensitivity so that the accelerator and the brake are detached from the car and become part of the driver's body so that each tremor is transformed into crystal-clear thought. It is not without reason that in the couplets, usually dismissed as being crude, inscribed on the front and back of vehicles, the vehicle is often cast in the role of the beloved; at their base is the living, breathing relationship between man and machine, and their pact to live and die as one.

At the Nechi Phu Pass, descending from a height of 6,000 feet, I often saw the Tata Sumo drifting down the gorge like a severed kite which the children standing at the bottom of the valley were waving to, imagining it to be a helicopter. Each time such an image rose in my mind, I would stare hard at the driver: Was my inner fear affecting him? But he would be in a deep trance; in a space and time in which his passengers had ceased existing.

From Bomdila—situated at a height of 7,500 feet—begins the play of clouds drifting about in an infinite variety. Fog suddenly obscures the world; in a while, the dazzlingly white Himalaya stands right in front. Bomdila is the headquarters of the West Kameng district, home to the Monpa, Sherdukpen, Aka, Miji and Bugun tribes. The dogs of Bomdila are infamous; they roam about on sub-zero nights and can take down a man and feed on his flesh. Such is the biodiversity that a truckload of one plant, the *Taxus baccata*, taken down to Guwahati, fetches enough money to buy a brand-new truck chassis. The *Taxus baccata* is a tall grass from which the anti-cancer agent Taxol is extracted in Kolkata and sent to Europe.

There was an old man in the Bomdila market who said in the manner of one demonstrating an invisible monument: 'The Chinese had marched down here during the war.'

I found a place to bed down in a slate-roofed dhaba in the Dirang valley. A mad wind sprang up in the falling evening and set up a wild whistling. The temperature dropped sharply and it was difficult to keep one's footing. Even though two quilts were piled up over my sleeping bag, the cold was boring into my bones. The mistress of the dhaba allowed me to move my sleeping bag close to the fireplace but before going to bed issued strict instructions to her terrifying dog, 'Keep sharp. No one must go outside!' I would stir slightly, moved by the desire to view the silvery Himalaya in moonlight, but the dog would grind its teeth and growl like an emperor: 'A fleeting pleasure for your eyes, or your life. Think well what it is that you want.' I would have to kill the desire within my heart and come back to my sleeping bag.

In the morning I made my way to a gompa—established by the Buddhist guru Padmasambhav in the eighth century inside an ancient fort, the Dirang dzong—to look for Lama Nawang Lamsang. In this area, which is culturally closer to Tibet than to India, Padmasambhav is known as Lopon Rimpoche. Young novice monks were seated in the sanctum sanctorum of that small gompa, reading from ancient scriptures. An elderly monk informed me that Lamsang was travelling outside the Dirang valley. After a moment's thought he opened a battered tin box, took out a very old piece of stone and placing it on my palm, said, 'This is the heart of a demon which was killed here. After it was killed, the Mon people converted to Buddhism.'

'How did its heart turn to stone?'

'What will it be if not a stone… It was a demon!'

There was no more reason left for me to doubt that symbol of the victory of Buddhism.

As one climbs up from Dirang towards Sela Pass, the vegetation thins out, disappears, and is replaced by snow-topped granite mountains and, in a few places, by densely growing grass which appears as soft as mattresses. Hidden in the dense fog, Army trucks scream and wail their way up in an ant-crawl; grazing yaks occasionally heave into view; the lack of oxygen makes breathing difficult. The Sela (13,700 feet) is the second-highest motorable pass in the world. These winding high roads, made possible by the prowess of the Border Roads Organization, resemble kite cord wound around one's fingers and then carelessly tossed aside. To the left, immediately after the Sela gate, was a lake which had frozen inwards from its shores. In the middle was clear blue water in which the universe itself was reflected. Some new Army recruits were playing with snowballs and taking pictures. From the window of a small, stone-hut teashop near the gate I could see valleys shimmering through gaps in the layers of cloud which covered them. A family made its living from the shop, selling tea to tourists and soldiers. Looking out at the soldiers, the tea-maker said sagely, vapour billowing from his mouth, 'The more difficult a place is to reach, the more its beauty becomes enhanced… But for how many days?'

The most reassuring sight in this bleak, mountain desert were the white flags which flapped restlessly in the icy wind. This is a custom in these parts: whenever one asks for something from the gods, he erects a white flag. Perhaps he lives with the conviction that his prayer will some day ride the winds to its intended address.

The driver slipped into a trance once more as the descent commenced. It had rained recently. The water dripping off the rocks and boulders on the sides of the road had pooled in the middle and frozen over, creating strange shapes, mostly like daggers. Greenery made an appearance after Jaswantgarh. In Jang, we stopped in an old Monpa house where a bottle of rum stood next to a kettle of water bubbling on a wood fire. A cat was perched on a stool next to the stove to keep count of the drinks consumed. The chimes which hung in the fronts of the houses were tinkling in the wind. The mistress of the house was sitting outside; she was convinced that life-threatening cold makes men honest.

We caught occasional glimpses of the golden roofs of the Tawang Monastery—one of the most important and famous centres of Mahayana Buddhism—in the falling twilight as our vehicle rounded corners in the road; the Collector had already been contacted and a grand suite had been booked in the Circuit House.

~

Gulping down pure mountain air in the pauses afforded to me by lungs which struggled in the thin atmosphere, I reached the monastery in the afternoon, looking for a lama who had returned from Sarnath. The spinning prayer-wheel mounted on the front gate was freezing. Teenaged monks were sitting in the lawn in front of the prayer-hall, eating porridge. The prayer-flag flapping in the wind was swaying the sixty-foot-high pole to which it was attached. Towards the monks' backs was the museum of this renowned monastery of the Mahayana Buddhist order. Among the exhibits were an enormous elephant tusk, ancient musical instruments, monks' belongings, and human skulls covered over with sculpted gold and silver leaf. There was also a library which included silk-wrapped religious manuscripts seven centuries old. The prayer-hall was awash in the glow of a statue of Buddha that had been brought from Tibet three hundred years earlier. On the walls were murals which depicted tantric rituals.

There used to be many legends about how such a massive statue reached Tawang. About half a century earlier, when a strong earthquake jolted the region, the statue split and many new stories were added to those legends. In 1997, His Holiness the Dalai Lama visited Tawang Monastery; on his orders, skilled sculptors were summoned from Nepal to restore the Buddha statue. During the restoration, certain documents were recovered from its belly. From them it was learnt that different parts of the Buddha statue had been carved separately in southern Tibet by adherents of the Gelugpa sect. These parts had been brought to Tawang on horseback.

I asked the lama in-charge of the museum why so many skulls were displayed. He pointed out Panden Lhamo, the guardian deity and protectoress of Tibet, in a mural and said, 'Earlier, lamas used them to offer liquor to the deities during tantric worship; but Pepsi or Coke is offered nowadays.'

'Where do you get that from?'

'From the general store in the bazaar!' the lama said, staring at me in astonishment.

After the Potala Palace in Lhasa, Tawang is the oldest monastery of the Mahayana order. It was established in the seventeenth century by the Merak Lama Lodre Gyatso. He is said to have been inspired and guided by his horse to do so. In the Tibetan language, Tawang means 'chosen by a horse'. Tawang is famous all over the world as a centre of Tantric worship; seventeen monasteries fall under its direct administration. Until not very long ago, tax-collectors from Tibet used to travel to villages in Tawang to collect land tax. China considers Tawang to be northern Tibet. It was on this basis that when Arunachal Pradesh became a state in the Indian union, China registered an official protest about India's claim on certain parts of the area. There are two pharmacies is the marketplace which exclusively stock medicines from the Tibetan system.

That evening in the bazaar, I met a robed monk astride a motorcycle. He told me that Jaspinder Narula would be performing at the Buddha Mahotsav festival. Udit Narayan had already performed there once. He also told me that the actors Shah Rukh Khan and Madhuri Dixit had visited during the shooting of *Koyla*. I asked the monk, 'Why is multinational Pepsi offered to the gods instead of homebrew?' He winked, and enjoying himself, replied, 'Buddhism is also a multinational religion, where's the problem!'

It was after he sped off with a roar of his bike that I understood how the monastic lives of these monks in this sparsely populated town at a height of 11,000 feet have irrevocably changed. Mobile SIM cards had reached a nunnery, the Gyangong Ani Gompa, two months earlier. Their texts, sent to friends in other nunneries, would remain suspended in the mists of the valleys for days on end. The other significant transformation in the nunneries and monasteries was the arrival of cable television. These structures whose silence had been broken for centuries only by the drone of thighbone trumpets now resounded with the animated chatter of monks discussing serials and films. A catchword from a jingle for a popular brand of motorbikes—Hoodibaba!—was then as much a hit among the lamas as it was among teenagers all over India. Television had brought in its wake its own episodic debates which run for years without pause. The elder monks believed that half-naked actresses and the violence in films would corrupt the celibates. The younger ones were convinced that a ban of any sort would compel them to watch television in secret; this would encourage the habit of lying and feelings of guilt. Television won out in the end, and the world of colour came into the colourless world of meditation and seeking.

The following day, Thondu, a teacher of novice monks at the monastery, took me to his room. He made me a cup of tea. In between the routines followed by a seeker, he told me that when His Holiness the Dalai Lama had visited the monastery, a few young monks had asked him, 'If Lord Buddha has proscribed liquor, why is it still used in prayer ceremonies?' The lord has decreed that black tea or fruit juice be used but, Pepsi, since it is easily available, has taken their place. Many old tantriks still use liquor but such practices are now being discouraged.

Shortly before the advent of television, there was a debate in the monastery: Should monks participate in party politics? T.G. Rimpoche, a monk connected to this monastery and considered to be an incarnation of Buddha, had contested for the Legislative Assembly seat from the constituency of Lumla and had twice been part of the government—even becoming minister—switching sides between parties headed by Mukut Mithi and Gegong Apang. The elders believed that politics could corrupt the renunciants; the younger lot requested that they should not let go of such a practical opportunity to serve the people. It was then that those babas from the Hindi-speaking belt who had reached Parliament on the BJP platform after the Ramjanmabhumi agitation of 1992 were presented as role models. This monastery alone had more than three hundred voters. All candidates from all parties would visit to canvass support during elections. Most of the monks from well-off backgrounds kept bikes and mobile phones. The number of lamas being lured away by the dazzle of materialism was increasing, but the administration of the monastery wasn't worried. Among the Monpa people, the middle son of any family with three sons is given up to the monastery. There was no shortage of new joinees.

~

The 24-kilometre road which connects Tinsukia with Duliajan was so terrible that travelling by jeep over it loosened all the nuts and bolts of my spine. That jeep belonged to a contractor who was travelling from Tinsukia to bring labourers from Duliajan. I travelled through lush green tea gardens to Kakojan and then to Nauhalia where the ULFA had begun its campaign of persecuting and killing Hindi-speakers on 22 October. This area, populated by the Matak and Moran tribes, is considered the ULFA stronghold. Every time rumours of ULFA chief Paresh Baruah's death do the rounds, he surfaces in one of the villages in this area to prove them wrong. According to the intelligence agencies, Paresh Baruah has many clones from among the Matak and Moran tribes who are kept in circulation so that the ULFA's extortion rackets run smoothly. Stories of how this militant-hero has become a legend are legion. A tribal said to me, 'A new wind will sweep this region the day Paresh Baruah ceases to exist.'

In Nauhalia was a small tunnel, enclosed within four walls, from which leapt flames. I had come especially to see this burning plume of natural gas which has long been presented as a symbol of the squandering of the natural resources of Assam. There were more than ten such spots in Duliajan, tunnels from which gas has been spewing for decades. The heavy smoke from the growling, burning gas hung far over the surrounding villages, and the night sky burned red with leaping tongues of flame. According to one broad estimate, 100 million cubic feet of gas is wasted each day in Assam. In terms of energy, 100 million cubic feet of gas is considered equivalent to 25 tonnes of petroleum. According to Oil India Corporation officer Prashant Barkakoty, it was important to burn the gas else it could lead to geological upheavals.

One fourth of the country's oil production is drawn from the wells in the state. One of the old political issues of the region is the miniscule royalty the Centre pays Assam in return for its oil. The slogan which precedes any anti-Delhi agitation goes like this: 'Delhi takes our tea, our oil, our coal. What does Delhi send in return: the Army!' The threat to puncture the pipeline which takes petroleum from Duliajan to the refinery in Barauni has become tokenistic and customary. Even students from the neighbourhood degree college use it to intimidate their principal during student elections.

~

That day I walked 11 kilometres without encountering a single truck. This was strange in an area which produced oil, coal and tea. I would carefully scan the wind for the roar of an engine but hear only the twittering of birds. After an hour, the waiting became intense and began to play tricks on me. Truck tyres ran riot on tree trunks and the haze growled like a live combustion engine. It felt as if the eyes of truck-drivers were speeding by me on the road. I would stamp my feet upon the ground and make certain I was on terra firma.

I finally found a tractor headed to Sibsagar. It was drawing a trolley on which were loaded nine goats and three sacks of rice; the trolley set up a musical chime each time the dried goat pellets rolled across its bed. A Nepali teenager sat among the goats and the bags of rice. The boy was a labourer working for an Assamese farmer. He had run away from his duties for two days to learn how to drive a tractor. The driver, Syedurrehman, had asked me to keep an eye on the boy so I began staring at him. He, too, was staring at me with unblinking eyes. The same slime which coursed between his nose and upper lip was smeared on the goats' snouts. When I finally lost the staring competition which we were engaged in, sitting on the rice sacks, I said to him, 'Why don't you wipe your nose?'

He stuck out the tip of his tongue, bleated exactly like a goat, and turned around to stare at the tea gardens. When the goats looked at him in astonishment, he glared at them in warning to heed their limits. When, in a little while, I made inaccurate attempts to bleat like a goat he laughed in pride and bleated a number of times.

I once used to know goat-speech but had now completely forgotten it. One more attempt on my part convinced him of his role as a specialist. Now, instead of long bleats, he emitted bleat-snippets so that I could practice and learn to talk like goats again. The animals looked on at us in astonishment. My ego of a reporter from Delhi prevented me from learning at such a fundamental level. He then began to look at me with his surly gaze.

After thinking long about how I might be of use, he said proprietorially, 'You have a cigarette on you.'

I pulled out tobacco from a pouch and rolled him a cigarette. He blew out smoke, contorting his mouth in many different ways, then went among the goats and, clutching at the tractor canopy for support, stood singing a song in Nepali. A three-way staring contest between the boy, the goats and I lasted until evening.

Syedurrehman finally dropped me off on a bridge over the Dikhu river on whose southern bank live the Borgohains (the secretaries) and whose eastern bank is inhabited by the Borphukans (the warriors). Sibsagar was a capital of the Ahom kings for 600 years before the British arrived. The British annexed Assam in return for repelling the attacks of the Moner (Burmese) occupiers. There is a profusion of statues in Sibsagar, all of great historical significance. For this, it is also now called the cultural capital of the state.

The layout of the Amravati Dharamshala, located in the middle of Sibsagar, was past my comprehension. Even though I was exhausted beyond belief, I measured the room with my hands. It was three feet wide and sixteen feet long. It was bisected down the middle by a slim bench on which an oil-lamp stood; the door didn't have a latch, the walls were studded with hundreds of nails, and a small round window opened up to the pond beyond. In the morning, my sleep was interrupted by hastily repressed, naughty, giggling voices. A number of children with colour on their hands were leaping about at the door but weren't entering the room. Holi had arrived.

The huge moss-, duck- and trash-filled pond next to the 300-year-old Shiv Mandir (Sivadol) in Sibsagar, constructed by Rani Ambika, was shimmering in the gentle breeze of Fagun and demonstrating evidence that it was a historical structure. A woman had cleaned her brass vessel and was about to fill it up with water when a boy chewing paan-masala spat into the pond. She was startled; the vessel slipped from her hands and started to sink. The past dazzles in the spit-stains of modern addictions and precipitates downwards; all historical places are destined to suffer the same fate.

Two boys were sitting on the stone steps leading down to the water playing a game, a primitive ancestor of Ludo, with tamarind seeds. When I asked them to accompany me to the Rang Ghar and play the same game there, they refused. The Rang Ghar, an amphitheater, was constructed by King Pramatta Singha in the seventeenth century for entertainment and for games. At the age at which he had this structure constructed, I used to offer my free services as a guide to white tourists in Benares. I stood a little apart from the two boys and uttered a mantra Shashwat had taught me: 'Alhamdulillaharabbiulalameen!' It seemed to have an effect. In a little while, Ranjit and Pehelwan agreed to come with me to the Rang Ghar in a Tempo.

The Rang Ghar was undergoing repairs commissioned by the government. Bihu, and the traditional buffalo fights, had not been organized in a long time and were unlikely to happen in future. The two boys knew that it was in this very Rang Ghar that the ULFA had been set up in 1979 by five boys who, like Ranjit and Pehelwan, would wander about its grounds. Some other boys were playing Holi in Talatal Ghar. They were chasing each other down and smearing colour. Talatal is a 250-year-old ruin underneath which is a tunnel that runs down to the Dikhu River. The queens would walk down the tunnel to the river for a bath and the king would use it in emergencies for escape. The walls, built with thin Lakhouri bricks, had paintings drawn upon them by Ghanshyam. Most of those paintings had faded and peeled away. Ghanshyam was the Muslim architect who created the Talatal Ghar. The ruins of his house can still be found on the bank of the Joysagar Lake. At present, the most current works of art included images of hearts, arrows, genitals and names scored into the plaster by the tips of keys. Ranjit, hiding himself slightly, wrote in many places: 'Reema, I love you.' Pehelwan had written Julie's name somewhere; lost in himself, he kept looking for it.

Both of them hesitated on the path leading in to

Vishnu Dol (a grand temple of which it is said that the British carried away its idol). Ranjit said regretfully, 'You go, we are Muslim.'

I tried to convince both for a while and then asked, 'Wasn't Ghanshyam Muslim?' Ranjit replied, unbending, 'Then the air was different. The air is different now.'

~

A rising moon; spring breeze; a window-seat in a night-bus; the tangled skeins of life which lose themselves among scores of unfamiliar tongues and finally straighten out among the activities which constitute living; racing hills; on the adjoining seat a Naga soldier with a caged rabbit going home on leave—what more can a traveller want! A little uncertainty, a little fear, a little adventure—all was there.

The bus was to reach Manipur the following day, via Karbi Anglong, Dimapur and Kohima. These names are uttered in the Northeast with such a sense of uncertainty that a picture of an underground life starts to form, one which remains invisible but which controls everything. Yet this uncertainty was nothing in the face of the mystery wrought by moonlight as it falls upon foliage so green it looks black. Like a mute film screen, unintelligible... but it feels... like ... anything can happen anytime. A stitch rises within as one looks on at the blue fog shrouding the deserted landscape.

At midnight we found a group of teenage girls soliciting in Jakhala Bandha. Their younger brothers and sisters were milling about around them. Whenever a girl would find a customer, the two would walk away hand in hand as if they were setting up a household in imitation of her parents. But, from the suppressed voices, the sounds of commerce and the beatings, it would seem as if the girl had transformed into a meagre hotel that was incapable of satisfying its customer's hungers. The Kaziranga National Park ranged alongside this highway; I crossed the park numerous times but never wanted to enter it. In the middle of dense foliage, bathed in the faint moonlight, the customer was the world-faamous Great One-Horned Rhinoceros and the girls were his feed.

The Numaligarh Refinery invaded my sleep like a great tower of light. The bus passed through an incandescent column and filled up with flammable material. A little further from on Kakojan was the Khatkati Petrol Pump where petrol and diesel were being sold from kiosks as carelessly as water would. Canisters and jerry-cans of fuel filled the bus, they were crammed underneath seats and in the aisles; everywhere but the carrier on the roof. A Naga co-passenger remarked that it smelt like Iraq inside the bus. Manipur shuts down often, trucks stop plying; this fuel is then black-marketed. This trade is the legacy of militancy and it provides livelihoods to hundreds of Manipuris.

Dimapur, Chumukedima, Kohima… At every large Army checkpost, the helper would run up to the sentry, hand him one fifty-rupee note and hurry back on the double. The bus would trundle on. Nothing was checked—Inner-Line permits, suspicious travellers, the jerry-cans and the containers. Most of the luxury night buses belonged to either prominent leaders or to officers who had people everywhere, and who had made all the right arrangements in the right places. Kohima was suspended in the sky and dozing. The city is really like the Milky Way—a sight Harish Chandola had wanted to show me on our previous trip. The bus would stop all at once; men would climb down to relieve themselves. Soon, it would seem as if silver cords connected to their navels were shimmering in the moonlight. Like they were nearly invisible kites being flown from a deep valley. This was the untrammeled pleasure of evacuation which was equally available to everyone in that terrifying battle-zone. But that casual freedom was the prerogative only of men. Women were deprived of the pleasure of carefree evacuation by their men who would perforce become their bodyguards.

The Senapati district of Manipur, which heaved into view in the dim light of dawn, saddened me. Dust was blowing about over naked barren hills in the cold wind. In places, new-growth elder trees stood like the teeth of a comb. One more day was about to begin in the poverty-stricken camps huddled around Army establishments. The Naga soldier sitting on the adjacent seat slipped out of his sleep and, easing the rabbit cage straddling his lap, lighted a cigarette. An elderly tribal woman wearing animal bones in her ears looked at him peacefully and, all at once, snatched the cigarette from his mouth and tossed it outside. Before the man could understand what was happening, she slapped him, all the while grumbling under her breath. The cage dropped from his lap on to the floor.

'You're sitting on cans of petrol and smoking! What does such a blind man do in the Army?' This must have been the gist of the woman's ceaseless grumbling. The rabbit, terrified by the many tumbles it had taken in its cage, was rubbing its forepaws in regret. The sun's rays fell upon its blinking eyes.

The burnt shells of eight oil tankers stood on National Highway 39 between the Korang and Kathi villages which had been set on fire by NSCN (IM) militants only two days earlier. Seven were overturned in a ditch, one was suspended upon a tree, its rear riddled with bullet holes. The tankers had been travelling single file when shots were fired upon them; afterwards they had been pushed into the ditch. One driver had been killed and fourteen people were injured. The Army camp of Maram was merely 1 kilometre from the scene of the arson and the killing; the flames would surely have been visible from there but no one seems to have interfered since, officially, there was a ceasefire between the Indian government and the Naga militants. A man who was carrying petrol from Numaligarh to black-market in Imphal told me that twenty-five tankers had been set afire in the previous two months. According to him, the Nagas hold Imphal to ransom because they control this highway. They shut down our supply lines at will, he went on, but every time they do so, my trade booms.

Surrounded on all sides by hills, Imphal is set in a fertile, egg-shaped valley to the east of which lies Burma. The hills to the north are inhabited by Naga tribes. The Kuki and the Mizo live on the hills to the south. Pangal Muslims who migrated and settled here three hundred years earlier live on the margins of the valley.

That morning, the cultivated parts of Senapati were full of jeans-clad women hoeing fields and grazing cattle. A lungi-clad woman was carrying breakfast to some of them on her cycle; the wrinkles on her cheeks quivered rhythmically with the rise and fall of the hilly roads. It is said that the game of polo was invented by horse-riders in this valley and it is the state-sport of Manipur. Manipur is the most ancient state in the Northeast. Its court chronicle, the *Cheitharol Kumbaba*, records the lineages of seventy-four Meitei kings whose origin is traced to the reign of the king Lairen Pakhangba in 33 BCE. Seven Meitei tribes of Tibeto-Burmese origin founded Kangleipak which is the ancient name of Manipur. The word Manipur came along with Vaishnavism in the eighteenth century which, for some time, also became the religion of the court. Today, as a reaction to the ongoing forced assimilation into the Indian mainstream, the Meitei are turning back to their ancient Mongol past, to the Sanmahi religion, their old calendars, their traditional dances, language and festivals. The struggle to free the ancient Kangla Palace from the Assam Rifles was underway. But there was also the fear that once freed, the palace would be sold off to builders who would convert it into multi-storey residential apartments and shopping malls.

~

I had three telephone numbers with me, none of which I could get through to. My legs were cramped after sitting for twenty hours in the bus. I went to Pintu Hotel, opposite the bus stand, to sleep. That evening, there were a great number of soldiers in the marketplace. Sporting competitions were taking place within neighbourhoods. The Meiteis have an abiding love for sport. In 1994, the Indian sepak takraw—a game which is played with a woven ball like volleyball but using both hands and feet—team wasn't sent to the Asian Games in Hiroshima because of lack of funds. Manipur was shut down in protest—all four members of the team were Manipuris.

The streets of Imphal would fall silent by 3 in the afternoon. Alcohol, speaking in Hindi as well as films and songs in the Hindi language had been banned by the militants. It is an old fashion in Imphal for men to wear face-masks and ply rickshaws. This was started two decades earlier by young, jobless graduates who were ashamed of the work they were doing. Other than visiting the memorials dedicated to the Nupi Lan, the Second World War and the war against the British, and surveying the Pintu Hotel, I had nothing to do.

The Nupi Lan (Women's War) happened in 1939, when the women of Manipur protested against their king and the British government by brandishing pestles used to husk paddy. They were revolting against the administration's decision to export rice from Manipur during a time of famine. Women cycle everywhere, and they wield an enormous influence in the affairs of society. The Meira Paibi (Bearers of Light), the traditional organization of women, meets by lamplight once the chores of the day are done. Alcohol was prohibited in the state under their pressure.

A driver, drunk, was enjoying himself in the basement of the Pintu Hotel. He took me along to a small room so that he could introduce me to his 'ideal man', Mahfouz Ali, who needed an audience for his long tale. In 1984, Ali ran away from his village in Rajasthan and reached Delhi where he plied a rickshaw. Everyday, he would ferry a gambler from a bar to a bus stand. Ali faithfully served the man for four years, and the gambler, pleased, got him a job in a transport company in Roshan Market. Ali reached Dimapur one fine day and began to smuggle timber. He now had four trucks and four wives—one Nepali, one Manipuri, one Assamese and one a traditional Muslim woman. He had given each one a house in four different provinces and numerous children. Ali was illiterate but had the right connections with the right people in the Army and in the government.

When the timber trade grew thin after the Supreme Court banned the felling of forests, he started to supply vehicles to the smugglers of Ukhrul grass. These vehicles—trucks, cars and jeeps—are re-designed in such a way that between 1.5 to 2 quintals of grass can be easily hidden in them. The Ukhrul grass is the famed Manipuri ganja which is much in demand in Europe.

The following day, I kept making the rounds of the offices of political parties. As soon as I entered the hotel that evening, Mahfouz Ali gestured towards the basement and said, 'We have a special today, from the Army canteen.'

When I got there in an hour, I found two carriers from Ara, in Bihar, and a Naga from Ukhrul sitting with Ali. The deal had more or less been sealed. The charade of using the final rounds of drinking to secure minor slivers of profit was going on. The carriers would keep stuffing 70,000 rupees in loose change into the Naga's jacket pocket and, each time, he would throw the money down on the table. The money would be sorted, crumpled notes straightened, the assurance given that the next time they did business he would be given a better deal, and the game of Stuff-and-Throw would begin again. When the Naga's pocket tore open in the drunken argument, he jumped up and challenged the two carriers to settle matters with fists instead of notes. When the two Biharis became heated too,

Ali sharply rebuked everyone and sealed the deal. The Naga then turned his attention to me. Swaying, he extended his glass towards me. 'Help, buddy!'

Old-fashioned Nagas consider turning down an offer of a drink insulting; thinking this, I drank from his glass. He kissed me on the cheek in gratitude. The consequence of allowing the rulebook to triumph over commonsense was that the man became insistent. He would press his glass to my lips every five minutes and exclaim, 'Help, buddy!' And plant a firm kiss on my cheek even before removing the glass. Ali would shout at him but he wouldn't stop. When nothing worked, the four of us escorted him out of the hotel. When he staggered off, some currency notes slipped out from his torn jacket pocket. Ali remarked on our way back, 'I was afraid he would bite you on the cheek and give you his AIDS.'

'Is he homosexual?'

'Who knows? He's never sober, or we would find out.'

AIDS is a widespread epidemic in the Northeast. I had visited an NGO that very same day where I met L. Dipak Singh. Singh was the first person I ever met in my life who confessed to being HIV positive. He promised to take me along to Churchandpur where incurable drug addicts are kept in chains.

~

The Vaishnavite of Manipur lives in reaction to the forced merger with India and to the high-handedness of the Centre. The king of Manipur signed the accord to become part of India on 11 August 1947. That same year, elections to the legislative assembly of the state were held under the Manipuri Constitution. The Praja Shanti Sabha, a coalition of parties opposed to a full merger with the Indian union, formed the first government under the leadership of Maharaja Kumar Priyavrat Singh. All the members of the ministry, including their royal leader, had Leftist leanings. The Left was on the rise at the time, in China, Burma and eastern India; Manipur could very well slip out of grasp. The Indian government exerted pressure upon the maharaja through the Manipur Congress—which had won twenty-four seats in the first elections—and, on 21 September 1949, got him to sign the Manipur Merger Document and dismissed the state government. It is said that the maharaja had been kept under house arrest. His demands to have the merger proposal passed by the assembly and to hold a plebiscite on the issue had been rejected. Irabot Singh, the maharaja's brother-in-law and a leader of the Krishak Sabha, went to Burma where he formed the Red Guard Army to struggle for the independent, socialist nation of Manipur. But he died of an illness two years later in 1951. There are many in Manipur who are named Lenin and Mao.

Two demands—to grant autonomy to the state and the other, to have it declared a Union Territory—were rejected. Even the status of a fully fledged state was granted only after an agitation that lasted twenty-three long years after the merger. Literature in the Manipuri language dates back 1,500 years but the language itself was included in the Eighth Schedule only in 1992. Meiteis cannot buy land in the hills due to local revenue laws but outsiders can own land in Imphal valley. The Meiteis, though a comparatively better-educated community, are counted among the Other

Backward Castes. However, since they do not receive as much reservations from the government as compared to the hill tribes, their representation in government jobs is lesser even though they are present in larger numbers. The relentless influx of Nepali, Bangladeshi and other outsiders (the myangs, as they are locally known) into the small Imphal valley has set a new hate simmering. Corruption among politicians, savage rates of unemployment among the youth and the regular shutting down of highways and streets are enough to ensure that the pot keeps brimming over. On an average, inflation in Imphal is 1.15 times that of the rest of the country.

Jawaharlal Nehru is the villain here. According to the Meiteis, it was Nehru who gave away Kabaw, a fertile valley 1,200 square kilometres in extent, to Burma, simply to build up his image as an international leader. For three hundred years—before the signing of the Yandaboo Treaty in 1826 at the conclusion of the Anglo-Burmese War—the rulers of the kingdom of Ava (Burma) and Manipur waged a continuous war over the Kabaw valley. This area, situated between the eastern part of Manipur and the Chindwin river in Burma, has changed hands many times from the fifteenth century to 1826 and has remained under the rule of either the king of Manipur or the king of Burma. In 1834, the British, in accordance with the wishes of their ruler, handed over Kabaw valley to the ruler of Ava and, as reparation to the king of Manipur, fixed an allowance. The Indian government continued to pay this allowance to Manipur until 1953 when Nehru called the Burmese prime minister U Nu to Imphal and officially handed over the valley to Burma.

The seeds of discontent which were sown at the time of the integration of Manipur with India began to bear fruit by the 1970s when a number of militant organizations with Leftist ideologies formed. In 1975, a young man called Nameirakpam Bisheshwar, a product of old-school Communism in Manipur, reached Lhasa via Nepal to be trained in the use of weapons. In three years he set up the People's Liberation Army (PLA) with some Meitei boys and attacked police outposts and began extorting money to put together a war fund. The PLA was the first such militant organization in the Northeast which rose above ethnic formations and claimed revolution through Marxism as its aim. Its strategies: the setting up of armed squads in villages and the siege of cities; the bringing together of all militant organizations of the Northeast and Burma to liberate Manipur from the 'bandit government of Delhi'. Soon after, Rajkumar Tulachandra and Maipak Sharma brought together city youth to set up the People's Revolutionary Party of Kangleipak (PREPAK), a guerilla unit, and K. Vinay set up the Kangleipak Communist Party. More than ten guerilla units were set up within two years and the words in red 'Outsiders, Leave Manipur!' began to make an appearance on walls. Imphal remained deserted even mid-afternoon, the Army began patrolling the streets, and the tribals were introduced to curfew. In September 1980, the Imphal valley was declared an area of unrest and brought under the Armed Forces (Assam and Manipur) Special Powers Act. Every winter, an anti-integration week is observed during which cable operators are forced to show an eight-minute-long film in which Manipuri law experts declare the integration to be illegal.

The Army apprehended Bisheshwar in 1981 from a PLA camp where he was lecturing young men on dialectical materialism. Seven of his chief aides were killed in that encounter. After four years, he contested elections while still in jail and reached the Legislative Assembly of Manipur as an independent candidate. Bishweshar's own comrades gunned him down, furious that he had accepted the Indian Constitution. The ambit of militant operations after Bishweshar's killing kept increasing. In May 1990, the United National Liberation Front (UNLF), the oldest militant organization in Manipur, along with NSCN (Khaplang), ULFA and the Kuki National Army, set up an all-Mongol coalition, the Indo-Burma Revolutionary Front. This made it easy for Meitei boys to find shelter after undergoing training in the jungles of Bangladesh and Burma, or after action.

The other savage face of violence in Manipur is to be seen in Naga-Kuki clashes in the hill areas. Hundreds of innocents have died in clashes between the NSCN (IM) and NSCN (Khaplang), most of which arise from issues of interference in Moreh and disagreements in matters extortion. This same blood-drenched game plays out in the Naga-inhabited areas of Burma where no one understands that an international border exists between the two countries. The NSCN has made an attempt on the life of Manipuri chief minister Rishang Keishing (who is himself a Naga). In 1993, the then governor, Lt General V.K. Nair tabled a report in Parliament, along with a recommendation that President's Rule be imposed in Manipur, which provided a sense of the situation on the ground: 'NSCN (IM) has occupied the Naga-inhabited hill districts of Manipur: Ukhrul, Chandel, Senapati and Tamenglong. This organization has deep ties with ULFA, as well as Hmar, Meitei and Burmese militant organizations which are all supported by the intelligence agencies of Bangladesh and Pakistan. They receive arms from Thailand and other countries in Southeast Asia. The NSCN intends to control National Highway 39 and Moreh, which is the centre of a money-minting drug-smuggling trade.' In May 1993, ninety-three people were killed in Pangal-Meitei riots. The Pangal Muslims constitute 7 per cent of the total population. Their organization, the Islamic Revolutionary Front (IRF) is already in existence.

~

The BJP coalition was in power in the state at the time. People from all over would visit the office of the ruling party with requests and appeals and it was a very good place to understand local politics. One day, I met a smart young man, S. Premanand, who had set his sights high in the profession of journalism. He is the son of the Madhumangal Sharma, a leader from the days of the language agitation, who had stopped eating rice for ten years in his struggle to have Manipuri recognized as a national language in the Eighth Schedule of the Indian Constitution. Madhumangal Sharma was murdered by the PLA in 1995 for his anti-Leftist views. Premanand had a scooter. We reached an agreement: I would pay for petrol and the two of us would interview prominent leaders together. One or a half litre of petrol would be bought at double the rate from an old woman in the market.

One afternoon, the two of us reached Mantripukhri to

interview Rishang Keishing—chief minister for a record thirteen years, a devotee of the Congress high command, and a Tanghkhul Naga. The meeting made one thing clear: It is futile to meet leaders, especially of the older generation, because they have fallen utterly out of context. They know the art of striking balances but lack all initiative. Keishing, considered a pastmaster at the machinations of the throne, had recently been ousted from power. The Speaker of the Legislative Assembly, Wahengbam Nipamacha Singh, had engineered a mass defection and made off with the chief ministership; at the time of our meeting, Keishing was the only MLA left in his party. When he was chief minister, the NSCN had fired a volley of bullets on his cavalcade and he had narrowly escaped with his life. The militant organizations had declared that after he died Keishing wouldn't find a grave within the boundaries of his native village Ukhrul. He was a regular attendee at church each Sunday and was waiting for Sonia Gandhi's order which would take him to the Rajya Sabha.

He made a few comments which everyone else would make, but he said them in a manner which made them seem very insightful. State politics is being managed in the same way as the underworld is; state leaders are even more dangerous than the militants; the richest people in the Northeast are underground but, before vanishing, they have silenced the most current questions related to the militancy. Thereafter, he said nothing more.

On our way out we looked carefully at the entrance gate to the back of which a thick metal sheet had been welded. A platoon of BSF jawans was deployed in front of it. Only two days earlier an Assam Rifles soldier and a girl had been blown to bits in a remote-controlled explosion there.

One day, dusk fell as I watched women kirtan-singers—sandalwood paste smeared from their foreheads to nose-tips—immersed in singing songs at the Govindji temple. I could understand nothing except the words Radha, Krishna and Vrindavan but there was a reassurance in their lovely soft voices, a reassurance which I then dearly craved.

Only a little while earlier, on asking the way to the temple in Hindi, a drunk man named Gyanendra Ningba had told me harshly that if I wanted to make it out of Imphal alive, I should forget the Hindi language. He was seated on a chair in the middle of the road. It was five, and no transport could be found. After walking for a long time I found that I had lost my way again. A nameplate stuck to the front of a bungalow bearing the name of the Speaker, Dr S. Dhananjay Singh, gleamed in the darkness. I thought I should invite myself in and ask him what a stranger stuck outdoors in Imphal after five in the evening must do to find his way home. Perhaps he would arrange transport to Pintu Hotel. The guards put me in touch over speakerphone. A boy came out and took me inside.

The smell of masala and dried fermented fish permeated the courtyard. A large karahi was mounted upon a gas stove. Many elderly women were grinding masala, cleaning rice and washing utensils. The Speaker was talking to Kuki C. Dangyul, the MLA from Saikul, holding a large sieve in his hand. He had a gamcha wrapped around his lower half, and was wearing an old red shirt unbuttoned. The Budget session was to begin the following day. There had been fisticuffs between MLAs in the Legislative Assembly in the previous session.

During introductions I came to know that Dangyul

owned a house in Moreh so I broached the possibility of spending a night there. In the middle of our conversation Dangyul took Singh by the arm and stepped aside. I could catch just three from among the gusts of words in a foreign language: Delhi, sincerity and Speaker. Perhaps he was giving the Speaker a piece of his mind for having appeared before a reporter from Delhi clad only in a gamcha.

Shrugging off the MLA's hand, the Speaker came up to me with a rustic swagger. He held one corner of the gamcha in hand and said in English, 'This our dress mean lungi.'

I said gravely, 'I am bowled over by your simplicity.'

Dangyul went into the drawing room and called Moreh. Some of S. Dhananjay's hangers-on were in there. Singh indicated with a wave of his hand and said in English, 'He telephone the Moreh for you.'

Further conversation was impossible because, all at once, he pointed out the door to the bathroom and said, 'Nature call the me so thoda jaldi.'

I thanked him and left. His younger brother Priyo Singh Graduate dropped me to Pintu Hotel in a car. That evening, the Speaker seemed to me a helpless rustic seated in the control room of a vast political machine, a man whose sole asset was his simplicity.

~

The museum in Moirang is an old neglected structure built upon the land of militancy. Inside it, placed upon upright stands, are rusted rifles, a cannon barrel, medals, helmets and a loudhailer—all of Second World War vintage—strewn about like sickles, hoes and sticks inside a farmer's house. The official effort at labelling history consisted of taking printouts on white sheets of paper and sticking them to the base of the exhibits. Outside the building, the following words were etched upon a stone: 'It was here that Colonel Shaukat Malik of the Azad Hind Fauj unfurled the tricolour for the first time on Indian soil on 19 April 1944'. A local told me that standing alongside Colonel Malik, and also holding the cord of the flag, was the handsome, mustachioed Mairembam Koireng Singh who joined the Congress and became MLA many times.

Because domination and a stern attitude are writ large on the facial expressions of the statues of Netaji Subhas Chandra Bose which stand in other parts of the country, he seems to be posing like a revolutionary character in a film. Here Netaji is lean, on his face are the hard lines etched by a life of war, and it bears the regret of defeat. If one gazes at him long enough, Netaji starts to look like the guerilla-ancestor of ULFA, NSCN, PREPAK, all of whom are fighting to liberate their homelands, aided by China, Pakistan and Bangladesh. He is a man standing within a jungle, in the middle of a battlefield, a source of inspiration whose battle-cry—'Give me your blood, and I'll give you freedom!'—each militant organization repeats today in its own language. A handful of people ranged against a colonial government, a handful of arms, countless dreams ... This is that same chemistry.

Bose had brought together all those Indian soldiers of the British Army who had surrendered before the Japanese forces in Singapore and Malaya to raise the Azad Hind Fauj. Of those Indian men and women living in Southeast Asia, who were roused by the dream of the nation's freedom, women handed over their ornaments and the men their lives. Most of these troops were Tamil whose fathers had been forcibly conscripted as labourers in rubber plantations by the British. An entire division of the Azad Hind Fauj had swept into the Imphal-Kohima war theatre with the Japanese Army which was driving the fleeing British forces before its. Their mission was to capture a piece of Indian territory and to unfurl their flag upon it. The rest of the war would have to be fought by the citizens of India. Their strategy was based upon a sentimental belief in patriotism which came to a naught. Azad Hind Fauj squads marching before the advancing Japanese Army would make an appeal in Urdu through loudhailers: 'All ye Hindustanis, quit fighting on the side of the English. Break ranks and join us. We shall liberate the nation.' The Indian soldiers in the British Army killed many of those making appeals on loudhailers during the battle for the Pallel airstrip in Manipur.

In March 1944, the three platoons of the Azad Hind Fauj which accompanied the 15th Division of the Japanese Army on its campaign to capture Imphal had three tasks assigned to them: translation, espionage and propaganda. Similar squads accompanied the 31st Division of the Japanese Army which was fighting in Kohima. After the decisive battle in the Northeast was fought, and the costs were counted, this is the picture which emerged: out of the 6,000 troops of the Azad Hind Fauj which were pressed into the Manipur campaign, only 2,600 could retreat and reach Burma. Out of these, 2,000 were sent straight to hospital. 600 were war casualties, 715 deserted, 800 surrendered and the rest perished to starvation and disease.

Major Fujihara, appointed liaison between the Azad Hind Fauj and the Japanese Army, had this to say in his memoir: 'The revolutionary army displayed satisfactory resolve but was inferior in terms of its officers' efficiencies, training and military capabilities. They lacked steadfastness and aggression.'

Fujihara, who was trained to see war from the point of view of a coach, forgets that this army had neither vehicles, nor wireless sets or sufficient rifles. Each time they would require a cannon, they would have to wait for the Japanese troops. An army such as this wins nothing, but it sets off a war within the consciousness of people that lasts centuries. To view a snippet of such a war, one need only ask this question in any crowded general compartment on any train in India: 'What might have happened had Subhas Chandra Bose been India's prime minister instead of Jawaharlal Nehru…'

~

There was a traffic jam. The carcass of a female sangai had been placed on a bench on the bank of the Loktak Lake with a garland of marigolds hanging from its neck. A board with English text written on it had been placed underneath the sangai's snout in such a way that it seemed outraged that its hunters had not yet been apprehended. The sangai is an endangered deer, numbering in the tens, which is found only in Manipur. The antlers of the male curve inwards and meet at a point to form a bow. In Manipuri, 'sa' is animal, and 'ngai' is to wait. This name comes from the deer's habit of stopping mid-flight and looking back. Until an officer arrived from Bishnupur to receive a memorandum and to offer reassurances, there was nothing to do but gaze at the islands on the Loktak Lake. Loktak receives water from five rivers: Imphal, Iril, Thoubal, Sekmai and Khuga. It was now our turn to wait.

The female sangai had been brought from the Keibul Lamjao National Park where it had most likely been hunted and killed. Spread over 40 square kilometres, this park is an island, made out of phumdi, floating on the Loktak Lake. Phumdi is formed when water plants, moss, mud and other plant matter combine to form a carpet around 2 to 15 feet thick. Hundreds of phumdi were floating upon the lake, spread out over 90 square kilometres, upon which fishermen's huts (phumdi shang) were built. Their fish-filled nets, floating underneath the surface of the lake, were to be pulled up once the order was given. More than fifty-five villages and neighbourhoods use this lake to obtain drinking water and close to one lakh people derive their livelihoods from it. One of Loktak's most intriguing features is that fishermen sleep in one location and after drifting all night, wake up in another. The Manipur government was preparing a marketing initiative to invite tourists from the world over to Loktak.

After talking among themselves about the trail of tears that dripped from the sangai's eyes, the occupants of the bus climbed up a nearby hill to gaze upon the phumdi islands drifting lazily in the wind upon the surface of the lake. Among those present was an elderly fisherman who gave us a much more plausible reason for the all-too-frequent deaths of the deer. According to him, the deer were dying of starvation because of a blunder made by the local administration. Earlier, when the lake dried up in summer, the phumdi would settle down in the lakebed and gather fresh earth upon which would grow the grass the deer fed on. Now excess water from the Loktak Hydroelectric Project was being released into the lake, and the phumdi would float upon the surface all year round. When they couldn't find grass, the deer would try to run off the islands and drown.

'You can either light a bulb or look at the deer. You can't do both together,' said the fisherman. The fisherman had no idea at all that he had captured the conflict between development and the environment with a flick of his fingers.

When the bus finally moved a girl commented, 'There are more NGOs than deer now, in a few days there will be no deer left and only NGOs will remain.'

~

I finally got through to a number and Bonomali, one of the foremost sculptors of Manipur, arrived.

Bonomali was as shy as ever but had transformed into a portrait of Dostoyevsky. He had a beard that hung down to his chest, sadness in his eyes, and a yellow tinge upon his complexion which looked like it had been daubed on with paint. The similarity was so striking that were Bonomali to be taken to Dostoyevsky's city of Petersburg, many souls would take human form and emerge to meet him. Ten years earlier, he was a student of fine arts in BHU and we lived in the same hostel. He had married his classmate Ruma Jain who was then teaching art in Silchar. He took me to his village, Khongman, which is outside Imphal. There he had set up an expansive workshop made out of straw on the bank of a pond where many artisans worked on a freelance basis. On the bank was a massive heap of rubble—a dream of creating the tallest terracotta sculpture in the world had come crashing down only a few days earlier. Inside, the artists slept on straw spread out on scaffolding; my stuff was kept there. Everywhere were strewn finished, unfinished statues, machines, canvases, many different kinds of kilns and implements which were all being pressed into service to express the times that we were living in. Dolen, a long-haired boy with rockstar looks, made life-like replicas of animals by hand which were much in demand in Delhi. He introduced me to a friend of his who, before writing to his lover, would get a leech to gorge itself on his blood and use it for an inkpot. The letters tended to be long, and this technique had been innovated so that he wouldn't run out of blood. The people of the village freely used the pond to bathe in; that same pond provided drinking water to the workshop. Many varieties of fish chutneys and local delicacies, food which the artists had brought from their homes, were to be had. One in particular, snails cooked with peas, had an unforgettable flavour. Any villager could tell from the torch lights bobbing about in the fields if militants were passing by or an Army patrol was making its rounds.

Bonomali's idealism hadn't yet evaporated. In between serious discussions about corruption, militancy and backwardness, he would plunge deep into sketching out the syllabus for an education system that would make students rational thinkers.

Bonomali took me to Andro, whose locally brewed liquor 'sui' is quite famous, where I saw a museum being born. There I met Motwa Bahadur, clad in a saffron lungi and dripping with sweat, who was engaged in building a Naga museum and a museum for dolls from the Northeast. Bamboo baskets, earthen vessels, animal horns, samples of dolls, traditional weapons, sheets, handheld fans were heaped about. He was happy that the militants weren't obstructing his work.

A tribal man kept fingering my bag for a long time. With full concentration he examined its structure, its stitching. All at once he fingered the scar on my head and asked a question which meant: How did you get this? This was a very special way of making introductions. Behind his hut bubbled a tin canister from which a very popular sui made its way down in drops through a pipe that was once connected to a bicycle pump. A girl served a glass each, still warm, for us to taste. I mixed the sui with water and drank it. The tribal man turned to Bonomali and said, 'What sort of a young man is he? He mixes it with water.' The next round I drank neat.

Bonomali went off to help Motwa Bahadur. I stayed there drinking and talking with an old woman until it was time for the last bus. The woman had a thick streak of kajal in her eyes and a half-smoked Panama cigarette stuck behind her ear. We didn't know even a single word of the other's language. Actually, we weren't in a place where there was any need for language. Merely the word 'sarap', said in different contexts and in different ways, is sometimes enough to convey feelings to the place for which they are intended. Sitting companionably with that old woman there, I encountered such conversations within myself as would have found expression nowhere else in the world.

'Bachchu, looks like you've had a lot to drink sitting with your grandmother!'

'Certainly not with my grandmother… Had I done so, everyone: my grandfather, my aunt, and my uncle, would have thrashed me.'

When I offered to pay for the drink, the woman glared at me with her black eyes so fiercely that I cowered like a small child. Instead, she gifted me a quarter bottle for the road. On my way back I touched a three-year-old boy on his cheek. He broke out weeping and howled: 'Myang… Myang!'

~

Sarungbai Nimai Singh was yet another Manipuri student of the sculpture department of BHU. He was fun-loving, extroverted and a little stubborn. On the first day of class, a classmate of Nimai's borrowed a chisel from him. When he came to return the chisel, Nimai refused to take it, saying, 'Tera hai, nahi lega.' (This is bent, I won't take it) That boy kept telling Nimai, 'Tera hai, mera nahi, le lo.' (This is yours, not mine, take it back) but he didn't. It was only after using many different languages that Nimai could convey to the boy that he had bent his chisel and he should have it straightened before returning it to him.

Singh had now become a lecturer in the arts college in Imphal. He had married a week earlier. His wife, a chandan streak running down from her forehead to the tip of her nose, would speak Hindi shyly. One day there was a party in his house in Yumnam Lekai. When we drank liquor to celebrate their wedding after the wedding albums had been seen, we found gritty sand in our mouths. The bottle had been dug up from a pit. When the grit was pointed out he said in his broken Hindi, 'Needs to be hidden away. UG people ask for scooter, say feed us, give us a place to sleep. Those elders who are their supporters, need to keep good relations with them...' A young man interrupted Nimai with a sly smile. 'The bottle is useful to maintain good relations.'

'If we separate, how we eat, how we clothe ourselves? What I am is because of studying in Benares. Study here, and I would be jobless. That these peoples won't understand na.' With great clarity, Nimai had put a finger on the conflict facing the new generation of Manipur.

~

Summer had arrived. A goat was grazing in the no-man's land measuring about 20 feet between India and Burma. On the other side, in Nampholang, children with tankha paste daubed on their cheeks for relief from heat were hawking red watermelon slices. Since sandalwood is expensive, only the well-off can afford to apply its paste. I tried to look for the sahuain and her daughters from the train in Moreh bazaar but had no luck. All at once a gang of Burmese beggars surrounded me in an alley. They roam about in India in the daytime and return to Burma in the evening. Those giving them alms must have been accruing eight times the merit because, in those days, that was how much the Indian rupee was fetching in Burma. This exchange rate runs the livelihoods of numerous families in Manipur. Many Manipuris buy plastic chairs, buckets, steel utensils, synthetic clothes, toys and articles of daily use from the Nampholang market—all of which are manufactured in

China, Thailand and other South Asian countries—and sell it for a profit. All the old women who were on the bus on our way back were accompanied by large packages and sacks. This is legal trade, and not even one-fiftieth of the underground trade in ammunition, drugs and teak.

During those days, militants were looting wayfarers on the road back to Moreh, and Ibai (Bonomali's brother-in-law) was accompanying me so that he could speak in Manipuri at the right time and tell attackers that we had nothing with us. Since an opportunity to play out his role didn't arise, he was happy and had gone off to a Meitei relative's house. Carrying the world-famous fragrance of the spices of South Asia in my nostrils, I reached a grand South Indian temple. The mridang was playing; an arati in honour of Vishnu was being conducted in Tamil amidst a riot of blue, yellow and green colours. I found out that about 17,000 Tamils have settled down in the area who, of all the people in the country, probably know the maximum number of languages. They come second after the Kuki tribe in terms of population. Since their business demands it, the Tamils speak fluent Burmese, Manipuri, Nagamese and Hindi other than the usual Tamil and English. They dominate both the overground and underground businesses. The other traders who are in lesser numbers than the Tamils are Marwari, Punjabi and Nepali.

Most Tamil families arrived here in the 1960s after fleeing the nationalization of industries by the Win government in Burma. The first batch had reached during the Second World War from Mandalay and Rangoon. It was during that period that Netaji Subhas Chandra Bose entered India through Moreh in 1944.

Earlier, it was the Kuki militants who would extort money from the traders but after the NSCN (I-M)'s attempts to extend dominance in Moreh, the tax had doubled and Kuki-Tamil clashes had begun. It all started in June 1995 after the NSCN (I-M) attacked a Kuki village. In retaliation, Kuki militants abducted a Tamil boy, suspecting him of being an informant working for the Nagas. After a week, a Tamil mob surrounded a Kuki village and set fire to it; they had information that the boy was hidden in the village. Kuki militants then attacked a Tamil neighbourhood and thirteen people lost their lives. Tension has continued since. There is a switch fitted in Moreh which regulates the violence. First the guerilla organizations battle each other to control the trade in smuggling; afterwards, Naga-Kuki clashes break out in Manipur, Nagaland, Mizoram and the Cachar areas of Assam which halt naturally, as a matter of course.

There was a large crowd of Indians at the International Bazaar in Nampholang. Every conceivable article was either being bought or sold there and the Burmese buyers were interested in handloom garments, medicines and bicycle parts. Due to their patience and sensual appeal, Nepali women are the best businesswomen here. I renewed my bag and my tattered T-shirt for very little money and then set off to explore the back streets of Nampholang from where the fragrance of Burma was wafting up to me. Indian currency was readily welcome and there were many Trekar-drivers calling out for passengers to Tamu.

A red-and-white bridge over a small river, half in India and half in Burma. After traversing a jungle which spanned perhaps 3 or 4 kilometres, a few strange-looking houses, which had neither walls nor windows, sprang up. There were small cabins in place of rooms, women working in kitchens and children playing could be seen from afar. There was a café, open from all sides, and in front of it were bundles of grass and wood. Grass-cutters, all of them old men and women, were seated at the tables inside. Here I came to know of a beautiful tradition. In most of these rural teahouses, tea is kept warm on tables; anyone can enjoy a glass or two for free and rest for a while.

A massive Buddhist pagoda stood in the wilderness. At the carved and decorated well outside the monastery, a monk in his robes stood washing a pair of jeans, beating it assiduously on the ground. I washed my hands and feet with water from a wooden bucket and asked him, 'Whose pants are you washing?'

'Mine.'

'You wear jeans?'

He raised his clean-shaven, heavy head and looked at me in astonishment. I didn't then know of the relatively liberal atmosphere prevalent in the monasteries there. Householders regularly don monk's robes, meditate, participate in the community activities of the monasteries, and then go back to their lives. This monk was a student who came everyday to practice vipassanna, a form of meditation. In the evenings, he would play guitar in a club to entertain the Japanese tourists visiting Tamu. His name was Mo, which means rain. He showed me a community grave near the monastery and said that many Japanese soldiers didn't return home after their defeat in Kohima. They committed hara kiri and slit their stomachs open. The Japanese tourists came there to see those graves.

Strolling around Tamu in the evening, he asked all at once, 'Are you here for the women?'

'Meaning?'

The gist of what he told me after a great deal of context-building was that Tamu has a very large whorehouse. And that the prostitutes there are classified not according to how attractive they appear to the buyer but according to the size of the buyer's ego. Because of the low exchange rate, afficionados from India come to Tamu to procure expensive prostitutes for lesser money.

I told him, 'I'm here to gather self-confidence to face my uncertainties.'

'This is what we are taught in the practice of vipassanna. A vipassi can even gaze at death as it arrives to carry him away and remain impassive.' Mo smiled as he commented upon the shared nature of our goals.

I didn't believe what he had told me about the prostitutes. Mo didn't say it but he sensed my disbelief. He took me to a long alleyway where he demonstrated that most of the prostitutes welcome Indian customers and cost a maximum of 20 rupees.

~

K. Bhawendra Sharma of Bishnupur was a bookworm. Sitting in Bonomali's workshop one day, he repeated the words of some ancient traveller many times, and said that the best way to see any place is through the eyes of a local resident. He was my eyes during my sojourn in the AIDS capital of India.

If one must travel to Churchandpur, and one's mouth is full of tamul, it is enough to merely raise four fingers.

The conductor on the private bus issued me a ticket with a suspicious smile. Number 4 is code for the heroin which is smuggled in from the Golden Triangle—Laos, Thailand, Burma—to Churchandpur via Moreh. The gangs of young men and women who dissolve the drug in water and shoot it have become one of the markers of this place. Their telltale signs are red eyes, a stony face and a mild fever. Manipur is ashamed of them, militants gun them down, they are kept chained up inside government and non-government deaddiction centres; yet their numbers keep rising. Up until then, 38,000 injecting drug users (IDUs) had been identified in the district and its surrounding areas. Protest marches with the slogan, 'We are not animals!' were being taken out by addicts and human rights organizations against the savage methods of de-addiction.

We visited the offices of three NGOs to find a user capable of talking about the deadly, difficult-to-overcome pull of drugs. It was being said there, unasked, that they keep no one chained up, that they distribute new sterile syringes, and administer oral substitution therapy (OST). Which meant that the hope of deaddiction had been lost; addicts were being taught to take alternative drugs orally so that the threat of AIDS could be contained. A girl who worked as a computer operator in an NGO told us, 'Go to a hot spot if you want the full story.'

There were four hot spots where addicts congregated. The going rate for Number 4 was 80 rupees per gram. Morphine and other drugs available in government hospitals and from 'our people'—as was commonly put— were a little cheaper. Spasmo Proxyvon (SP)—a morphine-derived analgesic administered to women during Caesarean deliveries—was banned but available on the black market. SP is dissolved in water and injected. A teenager was addressing three emaciated, addicted girls in the manner of an Opposition leader. His name was Chakchuk. ... No staff ... They eat our funds, admit over capacity... On top of that the government still hasn't been able to give Naloxone. Naloxone is a life-saving injection given to addicts who have overdosed. One of Chakchuk's eyes was in a continuous flutter.

I began my interview. 'How did you start taking dope?'

The twitching ceased. Chakchuk kept staring at me with that one eye and all at once spat out, his pupil dilated: 'Fuck off!'

~

Chalambi was proud that she and her child hadn't been found positive in any test administered to them. She had become an unwed mother at seventeen and didn't know who the child's father was, the man who had given her this baby one-and-a-half years earlier in exchange for Number 4. Her folks had refused to keep her. A relative had promised to set up a small general store for her so that she could support herself and her child and this promise made her happy. She wasn't prepared to accept that shared needles are the reason for the spread of AIDS in the Northeast. She said: 'Dealers first get the girls on the drug and then turn them into one-hit-per-session hookers. That's how the disease spreads.'

'Why didn't your family keep you?'

'They consider me a broken thing which shouldn't be kept at home... When the truth is that this little thing has been added.' She said this caressing her child, an emaciated thing with a big head.

'How does it feel to be high?'

She widened her eyes and spread out her palms. 'Like flying.'

'Does it feel the same even now?'

'Sometimes it feels like my child will die.' She admitted this after uncertainly touching one shoulder with her dry mouth and then the other.

Chalambi, who came from an exceedingly poverty-stricken household, picked up the habit from her elder sister who occasionally drank country liquor. Once high, the two sisters would laugh for hours. One day, a boy from high school gave them a taste of Number 4 so they could leave their troubles behind and fly. Her family found out two years later when she had begun to steal. Thereafter, she didn't know for certain how two years went by sleeping on the streets. But she knew the reality of paradise. She said, 'So many kinds of UGs… There's so much bloodshed all around that children grow up eating raw potatoes and start flying as soon as they're a little older.'

She told me that children ate raw potatoes before going to school so that the teacher wouldn't smell the country liquor on their breaths.

~

What a forest it was, flirting with terror!

A natural forest is a reaction, an alchemy in which flora, fauna and nature itself combine to evoke an ancient feeling of a shared life. We can understand only the effect it has upon us. It is impossible to grasp it in its entirety because it is a discrete, vast, impenetrable, forever-transforming life. The realization that one has been unable to gather within one's self even that slim glimmer of feeling puts such a stitch in the heart that everything becomes mysterious. The keening produced by two bamboo stems rubbing against each other distils in the wind to recreate, all at once, that lonely princess wailing in the wilderness whose story one had heard in childhood. The silence before and after the subdued cry of a bird at dawn leaves one in that state which a child must feel in this world soon after its birth. The rustle of leaves rotting on the ground send a river of fear thundering through the arteries and all the hair on one's body stands on end. Standing in an expanse of grass taller than oneself, time stops suddenly, an intense feeling of helplessness washes over, and man transforms into a transparent stain of the faintest colour on the spectrum.

Laimyum Dolendro Sharma and I were travelling on National Highway Number 44, on our way to Agartala. Laimyum was going to Tripura as the representative of the sculptors of Manipur at the Charukala fair being organized there. From there, we would go our separate ways. Travelling up to Silchar between small and mid-sized hills, we encountered forests—which can stand as a metaphor only to the deep mystery of life—all day. We sensed the presence of militants from the traffic jams we encountered in the wilderness. Vehicles speeding along on the deserted roads within forests would stop, reined in by some inner urge within their drivers, and the queues would keep extending. After a long wait some tribal in a distant hut would wave his arm—Yes, the road's clear. At that moment the gesture made by that man—the world's most strength-less, most left-behind—would acquire immense power because upon that gesture depended the being or the non-being of hundreds of lives. It was a momentary power that would be invested in that man by travellers hopelessly encircled from all sides, a power which he would wield with complete humanity.

At one place, it was the BSF which had caused a jam. Travellers stood in a line, their bags and briefcases held open. Each bag was searched.

We reached Silchar late in the night. Passing time was no problem at all. In speaking Hindi, Dolen would have to halt and be distracted so frequently that he would route imagination on to new circuits and take it on uncharted paths.

'You sweet is… We eat have… Our brother is… You embrace will… Absolute shadow become… Worry inside damage is…'

My email during those days was anil_jalebi@yahoo.com. He thought jalebi, that syrupy sweet which he had tasted before, was my second name. What he was saying was: You are my jalebi brother, I embrace you and will shadow you. Don't give in to worry, that will only harm you.

He was mad after new models of motorbikes. I told him: 'Where I come from, some people adorn their Bullet's handlebars with festoons and tassels, offer a garland to the headlight each morning and only kickstart the bike after having bowed their heads.'

He became sentimental… 'What good people… Give bike honour like mother.'

We took another bus via Karimganj to reach the Tripura

border from where vehicles would proceed further escorted either by an ROP (Road Opening Party) or by an Army convoy.

It was in the morning that Dolen got into real trouble because of his rock-star getup and his language. When the Army trucks full of machine-gun wielding soldiers were being positioned at the front of the convoy, at its back and in the middle, the passengers were made to stand once more on the side of the road and searched. In Dolen's bag were a number of hammers, chisels, drill machines, wire and other articles of the sculptor's trade. A BSF commandant, after raking through the articles, asked him for the identity papers which would prove him to be a resident of Manipur. After pretending to go through his pockets, Dolen said, 'Suppose that you were unemployed… A boy who cannot even buy handkerchief and gift to girlfriend… So which document would you show to prove Indian?'

The commandant grew even more suspicious. He took Dolen into a checkpost that stood a little apart and began interrogating him. '…You Indian people like that… Sending boys to jungle because harass…' I felt the tamul-spit in my mouth travel down my throat and a wave of disquiet surge up it. Dolen was getting angry. The matter could get out of hand. I hadn't used my fake press card in many days. I found it in my luggage and, holding my arms up, sprinted for the checkpost. I told the commandant, 'This man is my friend and a famous artist from Manipur, we're going for a programme to Agartala.' The invitation to the programme was in Dolen's pocket. He hadn't realized it in his anger.

~

That morning, no sooner than the convoy of buses—ringed in by the ROP—had begun crawling in Patharkandi that it stopped on a bridge over a river. The sound of multiple rounds being fired came to us from the jungle on our right, many grenades went off loudly and smoke began to rise from a nearby village. Boys bathing in the river and others from the villages nearby were running off to the scene shouting, 'Ambush… ambush!' In forty minutes, Army jeeps passed by in front of us, dripping blood. They were carrying three dead, four dying, a few injured people and, with them, scores of stupefied soldiers. They were being rushed to the hospital in Patharkandi. The journey had gotten off to a bloody, terrifying start and we were to remain waiting in that spot for hours.

This is routine for travellers in the Northeast. Very soon tea kettles began to clink underneath the windows and tamul-vendors set up their little boxes. An old tribal woman sold homebrewed liquor from a truck-tyre tube laden on her shoulder. Top-grade booze, guaranteed to magic away the fear of death itself, was available for 3 rupees per glass.

By the time the bus convoy moved post noon, the tragedy of Tripura had been articulated from different political angles in different local styles.

The grand palaces of tribal kings stand neglected in the forests of Tripura. At the time of Independence, the tribal population stood at 75 per cent of the total; these tribals are now a minority. Arable land, forests, politics and administration have passed into the hands of the Hindu refugees from Bangladesh who have periodically flooded into the state. The Kokborok language, Aamaar

Shonar Bangla—Our Golden Bangla—and the Aryan influence they represent, have taken over. Tribal militant organizations are fighting to take back their rights, Bengali militant organizations and the Anandamargis do battle with them. The last influx of Hindu refugees from Bangladesh had arrived in 1992 after the fall of the Babri Masjid in Ayodhya.

It was pure coincidence that when the convoy crossed the village, we saw soldiers driving six people before them. All of them had their hands tied behind their backs. There were being taken to a secret camp to be interrogated on suspicion of sheltering the militants. An armed soldier stood at every 20 metres right up to Agartala. The streets were deserted and we came across only the official convoy of the home minister of Tripura who was on his way to the hospital in Patharkandi to inspect the seven dead bodies. We were searched so often that by the time we reached Agartala in the night we had begun to feel as if we were sitting naked upon our seats.

~

Six rows of hills run north-west to south-east across Tripura, an infant's thumb embedded in Bangladesh and sandwiched between Mizoram and Meghalaya. On its western end, the strip of land extends south like the broadening blade of a machete. The chief tribes in the state are the Tripuri, Reang, Jamatia, Noatia and Halam, all of whom have been absorbed into the Hindu fold quite a while ago. The quest for a tribal identity gained momentum only later. Magh and Chakma Buddhists inhabit the state too. As do Mizos, Kuki and Garos, as well as some who still follow animist beliefs. Up until the fifteenth century, the domain of the monarch of Tripura, Dhanya Manikya, ranged between the Meghna river, the eastern border of Arakan and the Cachar region of Assam. Later kings joined the territories of Chittagong, Komilla, Noakhali and Chakla Roshnabad to the empire.

It was after the Bengal Diwani went to the British that Tripura shrank to its present proportions and extent. And it was after the emergence of communal politics before Independence that Hindus started to migrate from East Bengal. For them, Tripura was like paradise: the administration was Bengali as was the medium of instruction; Rabindranath Tagore, a poet dear to the palace, had composed paeans in praise of the state's beauty. The largest influx of refugees poured in in 1946 after the Noakhali riots; and after the formation of East Pakistan and the attacks on Hindus there in the 1960s. The proportion of the tribals in the total population went down to 28 per cent and the plains areas of Tripura became, for all practical purposes, Bengal. In 1941 the population was forty-nine per square kilometre which went up to 196 by 1981—the highest population density of all the hilly and mountainous tracts in the Northeast. The Congress and the Communists were ranged against each other as far as electoral politics was concerned. Tribals, dissatisfied with both factions, had brought into existence the militant agitation called Sengkrak (Closed Fist).

Inspired by the domination of Laldenga's Mizo National Front (MNF) in the adjoining state of Mizoram, armed tribals started attacking Bengalis living in border villages. One among them was a youth called Bijoy Kumar

Hrangkhawl who went to Chittagong to train with the MNF. On his return in 1978, he set up the Tribal National Volunteer Force and began attacks on Bengali villages and security forces. On the other side, an organization known as 'Amra Bangali'—inspired by the Anandamargis and supported by the Congress—had come into being. The tribals demanded the expelling of all aliens who had arrived before 15 October 1949. Their anger finally broke in 1980, after an innocuous incident, and became known as the Mandai Massacre in which, according to official figures, 600 people (sixty-nine among them tribals) were killed and 1,800 disappeared.

The tribals had begun the mass murder of Bengalis after rumours spread that a tribal boy had been stabbed in Lambucheda village near Agartala. Three hundred people were killed in the Mandai market alone, 34,600 houses were torched and 3 lakh people fled into refugee camps. There has been no governmental investigation of this violence even to this day. The media has always pointed to Bijoy Kumar Hrangkhawl as the orchestrator of the massacre.

Around this time, the Bangladeshi government started the process of settling Muslims from the plains in the Chittagong hills. After violent clashes between security forces and the Chakma Shanti Vahini, 70,000 Chakmas fled to Tripura where they were housed in six camps. While a few thousand have returned home to Bangladesh, about 5,500 still remain. Locals fear that if the government continues to provide Chakmas with rations, education and other facilities, they will never go back.

In 1988—after Laldenga became chief minister of

Mizoram following an agreement with Rajiv Gandhi—Bijoy Kumar Hrangkhawl was put on a plane along with his family, flown to Delhi, hosted in a five-star hotel and, after he put his signature on a peace treaty, presented to the media. As part of the deal, said the government, it would make utmost effort to identify illegal immigrants and return their land to tribals. The agreement has since remained on paper. Bijoy Hrangkhwal is today chairman of the Tripura Rehabilitation Plantation Corporation Limited which works to rehabilitate militants. He travels with security provided by the government. After his surrender more than a dozen militant organizations who have the backing of the Congress and the Communist Party—the two political formations that alternately rule Tripura—have mushroomed in the state. The abduction of truck-drivers, extortion, rape and violent encounters with security forces are common. Eight hundred and thirty-nine kilometres of the 1,001 kilometre-long Tripuri border is with Bangladesh. The first town in Bangladesh is a mere 2 kilometres from Agartala. The regular traffic of labourers from Bangladesh, in collusion with security forces, is an everyday occurrence.

The local Kokborok language has been written in the Bengali script from the maharaja's time. The tribals want it replaced by the Roman script. In the opinion of the Kolkata-based Institute of Language and Applied Linguistics—which conducts research on developing scripts for the country's tribal languages—the robust, well-researched Bengali script is best for the Kokborok language. According to them, with the use of the script, Bengalis will learn the tribal language too, and this will lead to integration in society. The tribals hold that with the use of the Roman script, children will become proficient in English; this will stand them in good stead in the job market and will help them interact better with the world. The political battles in Tripura may be understood from this difference.

~

It is said that Sachin Dev Burman, maddened by his love for music, fled home with a harmonium. A grand statue of his stands in Agartala. While I was gazing upon him, Dolen wrote my name in the register meant for artists attending the Charukala Mela in Rabindra Bhawan, my bag was taken away and kept in a room in the guest house. When I made a half-hearted protest, Dolen said, 'Jalebi brother, you keep shut mouth for little and will become real artist.' He took a packet of M-Seal—an adhesive commonly used to plug holes in pipes—from his bag. In half an hour he had fashioned a smiling goat and a playful dog. Thereafter he took me to the organizer's house, a man who was the principal of an art college. He gave the two figurines to the man's wife and, smiling shyly, said, 'We made this with lot of love and brought for you.'

We remained high on the list of VIP guests for the following week only because of Dolen's guileless, soft countenance. He would work in the daytime and I would roam. The inner worlds of the gathered artists would open up in the evenings. There were two addas frequented by Bengalis near Rabindra Bhawan; their chief occupation in the addas was the criticism of the Bengalis of Kolkata. According to them, Kolkata has been culturally corrupted.

The city has been sold off to the Marwaris, they claimed; the chief symptom of this was the forsaking of the afternoon siesta by the Bengalis in pursuit of money. This was how, they said, that the 'siesta similarity' which Bengal enjoyed with the revolution-loving countries of Latin America had been ended. Such vainglorious overstatements would frequently pepper conversations.

A carefree painter from Kolkata, Baghan Das, was also attending the mela. Many stories from tribal areas would drip in a continuous stream from his beard, which started from underneath his calm eyes and flowed down to his stomach. He had travelled everywhere in search of subjects and new art forms, especially to those areas where Naxalite agitations are taking place. He had also made unsuccessful efforts to conserve Santhali art, especially from those areas near Santiniketan; as well as the work of the sculptor Ramkinkar Baij. One night I said to him, 'The subject and the means of expression are what determine the life of an artist; to declare that one is on a quest for them is a marketing gimmick. Tell me truthfully, why do you go wandering among tribals?' He smiled mischievously. Then, for three nights straight, he told me of his childhood spent in a forest in Assam.

On the first night, the boy saw a train. He watched it for many years, staying hidden in the forest. He could not stop wondering how the train ran. Where in the unknown yonder did the train go, screaming chuk-chuk! And, before returning, where did it leave the many people who were inside it?

On the second night, the boy kept a tortoise in a pond which had four oars around itself. After a wait of many days, the tortoise would lift its head once and say, you need nothing else but your will to sail all the seas of the world; that same will which moves my oars.

On the third night, the child saw a rainbow and, for the rest of his life, remained stunned by the anarchy of colours.

On the fourth night I said, 'You should sing that joint effort by Ghalib and Gulzar: "The heart seeks once more those carefree days and carefree nights".'

'How did you know? That is a song dear to me.'

Wandering about, he would seek that mental and emotional state in which he could enter the subject and take on its mantle of thought. That which appeared on the canvas at the end of this process, critics would call 'Abstraction'.

~

Upon viewing most of the historical structures of Tripura, two things—the stamp of Bengali culture, and the anger of the tribals—become simultaneously clear. The tribals of Tripura claim that magnificent palace, which is now the Legislative Assembly of Tripura, as the final symbol of their pride and demand that the government vacate it. Rabindranath Tagore had prevailed upon a bank to secure the loan required to build the palace and had also christened it Ujjayanta Mahal. Many intellectuals from Bengal, including the scientist Jagadish Chandra Bose, would come to the palace to stay.

It was after the old palace was razed to the ground by the great earthquake of 1897 that King Radhakishor Manikya had the Ujjayanta Mahal built. Since funds in the treasury were low, Rabindranath Tagore had not only gotten the king a loan of 1,50,000 rupees from the Bengal Bank in Kolkata, but also had the construction contract granted to Martin and Burn Company.

The tribals commonly complain that in the eyes and the manner of the Bengali tourist from Kolkata, as he looks at the palace, is the pride of having taught them to climb down from their trees and live in houses.

~

We eventually become like those whom we hate. Seated on a carved sofa in his home, Bijoy Kumar Hrangkhawl was the spitting image of a rural Bengali schoolmaster. He had pulled together many tribal organizations to form the Indigenous Peoples Front of Tripura. Two years earlier he had been chosen MLA from the Kulai seat in north Tripura. At that time his demand was the imposition of the Inner Line Permit, as it is applied in Arunachal Pradesh and Nagaland, in Tripura so that usurpation by outsiders could be halted. According to the Communists, his surrender was a sham; he still kept the militants in his pockets and would still use them.

I asked, 'The militants may carry out as many massacres as they can, but is it possible to erase the Bengali history of Tripura?'

He smashed a fist into the palm of his other hand and exclaimed, 'But where's the logic in celebrating that history and destroying one's future with one's own hands?'

He was truly a man with a one-track mind and a clear agenda—land was scarce and the population vast; the tribals would do everything in their power to secure their lives and their progress in Tripura. But underneath this resolve was the rubber plant which, in the coming days, could become a representative symbol of the red soil of Tripura.

Bijoy was chairman of the Tripura Rehabilitation Plantation Corporation Limited which was settling militants and jhum cultivators on rubber plantations between 1 and 4 hectares in size. Jhum cultivation yields little and land, too, deteriorates speedily. The Rubber Board was offering a grant of 5,000 rupees per hectare along with plants, training and equipment. The Rubber Board, working under one more programme sponsored by the government, was taking tribal land on seven-year leases and putting down plantations. The workers were the owners of the land who, after being taught the finer points of planting and marketing, would be granted the rubber estate along with the gift of a processing unit. At that time Tripura had rubber plantations spread out over close to 20,000 hectares and, in terms of production, the state had become second, after Kerala. The Rubber Board had set up many projects to manufacture surgical gloves, sandals, tyres and rubber bands which were to begin production in the coming days.

In an ongoing experiment, 2 per cent latex was being mixed with a hundred kilogrammes of bitumen to build rubber road surfaces. It has been found that in areas with high rainfall, rubber-surfaced roads last thrice as long as normal roads. This technique had been imported from America where 20 per cent of all the roads have been rubberized. The road in front of the Rubber Board office had also been rubberized to build faith in the technique.

Before the 1980s, rubber was a wild tree growing in the

jungles of Tripura which even the forestry department had categorized on paper as a weed. When the Rubber Board would set up the plantations, the militants, in the time-honoured fashion of wreaking vengeance upon government property, would destroy them. The cancellation of the project itself was considered many times. It was that same rubber which was coming to the aid of the militants by helping in their rehabilitation. Bijoy Kumar Hrangkhawl told me that very few people of India know that about half the honey produced in the country comes from rubber plantations. Bees are attracted to flowers of the rubber plants. An average of 2 quintals of honey is prepared from a plantation 1 hectare in size.

Hinting at the militants and their pasts, I asked Bijoy, 'Those bees which alight upon rubber flowers, don't their stings fall off?'

He kept laughing for a long time at this question of mine.

ACKNOWLEDGEMENTS

The following books, journals and documents were consulted in the writing of this account:

Nari Rustomji, *Imperilled Frontiers: India's North-eastern Borderlands* (Delhi: OUP, 1983); Arup Kumar Dutta, *Cha-Garam: The Tea Story* (Delhi: Paloma Publications, 1992); *Brewed in the Sweat of Forced Labour: A Fact Finding Report on the Conditions of Tea Plantation Labour in West Bengal and Assam*, National Campaign on Labour Rights, made available to me by Subhash Sen of Tinsukia; the Census Reports of Assam, 1971 and 1991, and of Tripura, 1971 and 1981; *Agricultural Atlas of Assam*, Faculty of Agriculture, Assam Agricultural University, Jorhat, 1983; Centre for Science and Environment, *Floods, Floodplains and Environmental Myths* (Delhi, Centre for Science and Environment, 1990); Amalendu Guha, *Planter Raj to Swaraj: Freedom Struggle and Nationalist Politics in Assam 1826-1946* (Delhi: People's Publishing House, 1977; B.G. Verghese, *India's Northeast Resurgent: Ethnicity, Insurgency, Governance, Development* (Delhi: Konark Publishers, 1996); Sanjoy Hazarika, *Strangers of the Mist: Tales of War and Peace from India's Northeast* (Delhi: Penguin, 2000); Prafulla Kumar Mahanta, *The Tussle between Citizens and*

Foreigners in Assam (Delhi: Vikas, 1994); *Northeastern Coalfields: Northeastern Coalfields at a Glance* (Guwahati: Coal India Limited, 1994); Nirmal Nibedon, *The Night of the Guerillas* (Delhi: Lancers Publishers, 1987); Verrier Elwin, *Myths of the Northeast Frontier of India* (Shillong: North East Frontier Agency, 1958); Verrier Elwin, *A Philosophy for NEFA (North East Frontier Agency)* (Shillong: North East Frontier Agency, 1959); M. Horam, *The Nagas and Their Origin* (Kohima: The Thinker, 1974); Harishchandra Chandola, *Naga Katha* (Meerut: Samvad Prakashan, 2009); Y.D. Gundevia, *War and Peace in Nagaland* (Dehradun: Palit and Palit, 1975; Manifesto of the National Socialist Council of Nagaland; Laldenga, *Mizoram Marches Towards Freedom* (Mizoram: Publicity Department, Underground Government of Mizoram, 1970; Priyavrat Singh Maharajkumar, *Reminiscenses of the First and Last Chief Minister (Under Manipur State Constitution) in Manipur: Past and Present*, Sanjoba (ed.) (Delhi: N. Mittal Publications, 1988); K.S. Singh, *The People of India: An Introduction*, National Series, Volume 1 (Calcutta: Seagull Books, 1992); *The People of India: Scheduled Tribes*, National Series, Volume 3 (Delhi: Oxford University Press, 1994; Bertil Lintner, 'Indo-Burmese Frontier: A Legacy of Violence', *Jane's Intelligence Review* Volume 6, Number 1, London, 1994.

~

I am grateful to late Bhrigu Kumar Phukan, one of the leaders of the Assam Andolan and former state home minister; Satyanand Pathak, editor of the *Purvanchal Prahari*, Guwahati; and Ravishankar Ravi, senior journalist, for the information which they generously provided. I am especially obliged to S.K. Tiwari, former chief secretary of Meghalaya, for his amendments of my factual and linguistic shortcomings.

www.ingramcontent.com/pod-product-compliance
Lightning Source LLC
Chambersburg PA
CBHW061937220426
43662CB00012B/1936